All you need for
Christmas

A resource book for primary schools

Edited by David Day

All you need for Christmas

Contents

Stories

Plays

Assemblies

Carols and songs

Worksheets and activities

Games and fun

Planning templates

Did you know...?

The Christmas story 1

The Christmas story is often told in different ways for new audiences. David Day has written this simple and engaging version especially for Key Stage 1 children.

Mary's amazing message from God

A long time ago there was a girl called Mary. She was very, very good. In fact, she was *so good* that God picked her to do a really important job. He wanted her to be the mother of Jesus, so he sent an angel to tell her the news.

Well, Mary was sleeping. You know what it's like when you wake up in the night, don't you? At first you don't know what's going on. The angel was standing in her room dressed all in white, just like a washing powder advert, and Mary was scared. (Wouldn't you be?) But the angel told her not to be frightened and she calmed down.

'I've been sent by God, Mary,' he began. 'There's nothing to worry about. God wants you to do a special job because he knows you're so good. He wants you to be the mother of a very special baby.'

'B... b... baby?' echoed Mary. A thousand thoughts raced through her head, but the angel explained that the baby would be the Son of God, and that he should be called Jesus. He would be a great king and would reign forever.

Well, this was too much for Mary to take in at night. It had all happened too quickly.

She was excited, but also still a little frightened. She knew she had to obey God's wishes.

'Of course I'll do what God wants. I'm his servant,' she said and the angel smiled and left her. Mary kneeled down and prayed, thanking God that she had been chosen.

Later, she told Joseph all about it. He was a good man and was already engaged to Mary. They got married and lived in a town called Nazareth. They were very happy and the baby slowly grew inside Mary.

A long journey

Then came bad news. The ruler of the land – the Roman Emperor – wanted to count everyone to make sure they all paid their taxes. He ordered that on a certain day everyone would have to go to the place their family had come from to be counted. Afterwards, they could go home again. Joseph's family had come from Bethlehem, many miles away. Well, that wouldn't be a problem these days, but Mary and Joseph didn't have a car, or a bus they could catch. They had to walk for days and days, and the baby inside Mary was really big now and she got tired easily. But she didn't complain as Joseph led the way along rough paths that went up hills and down into valleys. At night they slept under the stars, sometimes around a campfire with other people.

After a while, Joseph became concerned because Mary was very tired, and so he made her ride on the donkey that carried their food and water. Even that wasn't very comfortable. Have you ever ridden on a donkey?

★ **Stories**

Nowhere to stay

As they neared Bethlehem, Mary was dreaming of a lovely comfortable bed, only to find that the place was full of people all there for the census – the counting. Every single room was full!

'Oh, goodness me!' thought Joseph. 'What am I going to do? Mary's got to have somewhere to sleep!' He knocked on door after door and was very worried by the time he tried the last door in the street – the only one he hadn't knocked on.

Now – you've got to understand that everyone was knocking on doors asking for rooms, so the owners were getting a bit fed up. This particular innkeeper had been to the door many times and was a bit short with Joseph.

'No. No room. Sorry,' was all he said.

'But…' began Joseph.

'Sorry. Can't do anything about it,' said the innkeeper. 'Blame the Emperor. It's his fault.'

'But my wife's about to have a baby!' Joseph blurted out. 'We've nowhere to go and we must have shelter…'

'A baby?' asked the innkeeper. 'Why didn't you say!' He stood still and rubbed his chin. 'All I can offer you is a stable. I can get some fresh straw and…'

'Thank you!' cried Joseph with a smile.

'Thank you very much. I'll get my wife.'

'And I'll get mine to come and help,' replied the innkeeper, but Joseph had already gone and he was talking to an empty doorway.

Two minutes later, Joseph came back with Mary and the innkeeper and his wife fussed around her, making her as comfortable as could be.

Within seconds she was fast asleep, but not for long, because the baby was born soon after. Mary named him Jesus, just as the angel had told her to.

The shepherds and the angel

Around Bethlehem there were many hills and on most there were sheep with groups of shepherds looking after them. One group of shepherds was sitting around a warming fire, chatting about this and that. Suddenly, the angel appeared to them and they were very frightened. The angel calmed them down and told them his wonderful news.

'A special baby has been born in Bethlehem,' he told the open-mouthed shepherds. 'This baby is the Son of God – the King who has been promised by God. He is in a stable, lying in a manger. Go and worship him!'

Imagine how excited the shepherds were after they heard that. They all wanted to charge off down the hill but first they had to decide which of them would stay and protect the flocks.

They also knew they should take a gift and this worried them – they didn't have much money. At last one of them suggested taking a lamb as their present and the others thought this was a great idea. A new-born lamb for a new-born baby! So, having chosen a lamb, they set off to find the Son of God.

Stories ✪

They had to be careful because on the hillside it was dark and stony with thorny plants hidden in the shadows. They arrived in Bethlehem a little out of breath and began to ask about a new baby. Well, word gets around quickly and it didn't take too long to find the stable where the baby Jesus was lying in a manger. They kneeled down and gave their gift to Joseph. After all, Jesus couldn't hold it for himself yet, could he!

Joseph and Mary said thank you and they chatted for a bit. Then the shepherds left because they were worried about the sheep. Jesus had had his first group of visitors, but more were on the way.

The Three Wise Men

Three very clever men from faraway lands had been told by their astrologers that a new king would be born and they were already travelling to find him. They didn't see an angel but a special star guided them every night so that they didn't get lost.

After travelling a long time they were close to Jesus, but they were about to make a dangerous mistake. 'Kings,' they thought, 'are always born in palaces,' and so when they reached Jerusalem they visited King Herod. They told him about the star, the birth of a new king and asked if they could see the baby.

Herod was amazed. He didn't have a baby son. Suddenly he realised that a new king might be a danger to him. The people might like the new king more than him! Swiftly, he thought up a clever plan.

'Tell you what,' he said to his three visitors. 'You go and find this little baby and then come back here before you go home. You can tell me where he is so that I can go and give him a present as well.'

The Three Wise Men thought this was a good idea and went on their way, still following the star. At last it stopped over a little inn in Bethlehem. The Wise Men went in and found the baby Jesus. He didn't look like a king, but they believed what they had been told. They gave Mary and Joseph presents for the boy to have when he was older, and after a while they left the room and climbed back on their camels. They were full of joy at what they'd seen but they decided that they did not trust King Herod, so they went back to their own lands without stopping to see him.

Herod went purple in the face with rage when he found that they had tricked him. He sent out his soldiers to find this new king and kill him, but he was too late. By then, Mary and Joseph had taken Jesus many miles away, where they would be safe.

⊗ **Stories**

The Christmas story 2

> **T**he Christmas story is not always told in its entirety. Here is a new full version of it, told for Key Stage 2 children by children's author Joan Carlyon.

Part 1

Two thousand years ago, in the land we now call Israel, there lived a young woman called Mary. Mary was an ordinary girl who lived with her mother and father in an ordinary house in Nazareth, a city in Galilee.

In those days, Jewish girls married young and their husbands-to-be were chosen by their parents. And so it had been arranged for Mary to marry a man called Joseph, the local carpenter. There was a lot to do before the wedding and many decisions to be made. Which date should they choose? Who should they invite? What should they wear? And most importantly, what should they eat? After the marriage ceremony, there would be a torch-light procession and a wedding feast which could last for days.

Plans were being made but, meanwhile, like the rest of her unmarried friends, Mary stayed at home and helped her mother with housework.

Like lots of ordinary people, Mary was clever and hardworking. Every day, she would help her mum to bake the unleavened bread, cook a tasty dinner, sweep and clean the house, and fetch water from the well in the tall pitcher jar which she'd learned to carry balanced on her head. When all the housework was done,

Mary liked to sit in the quiet of the house and spin the soft wool that the shepherds sheared from the sheep they kept on the hillsides outside the city walls.

One day, Mary was sitting on her own, spinning wool. She was thinking about her coming wedding and all the things she had to do before her marriage, when suddenly, without warning, an angel appeared. He just appeared out of nowhere and stood there, in front of her. She almost jumped out of her skin.

'Don't be afraid, Mary,' said the stranger. 'I'm the angel Gabriel and I've a message for you from God.'

At first, Mary thought she was imagining things. Why would God send her a message? She was just an ordinary girl.

'You've been specially chosen,' said the angel. 'God has sent me to tell you that you are going to have a baby. You must name him Jesus and he will be the new King whose reign will last for ever and ever.'

Mary was amazed. 'There must be some mistake,' she said. 'I'm engaged to Joseph but we're not married yet. How can this happen?'

'Don't worry,' said the angel. 'God can do anything. You will be the mother of a very special baby. Your child will be the Son of God.'

When Mary heard what the angel had to say, she had a feeling that everything would turn out right. 'I'll do whatever you ask,' she said to the angel, 'and I'll put my trust in God.' Then the angel vanished, and Mary was left alone.

Soon after the angel's visit, Mary decided to go and stay with her cousin, Elizabeth, who was married to a priest named Zechariah and who was also expecting a

Stories ✪

baby. It was a long journey for Mary because Elizabeth and Zechariah lived in a town a long way from Nazareth, far away in the hills of Judaea.

After days of travelling, Mary arrived at her cousin's house. She was tired and stiff after her long, dusty journey, but the moment she saw Elizabeth, she was bursting to tell her the fantastic news.

'God bless you, Mary,' cried Elizabeth as soon as Mary had told her. 'You're going to be the mother of our Lord. It's fantastic! I can't tell you how thrilled I am that you've come to visit me. The moment I heard your voice, I felt the baby jump in my womb. You are certainly something special. You put your trust in God and he's kept his promise.'

Excitement and happiness bubbled up inside Mary and she started to sing. Imagine that! All those words of love and joy and thanks began to spill out of her. Mary sang like a bird, in praise of God, and when she had finished, she and Elizabeth sat down to tell each other all their news.

Part 2

Elizabeth had a lot to tell. Some very strange things had happened to her and Zechariah recently. But she didn't want to rush her story. If Mary was going to understand any of it, it was better to hear it from the very beginning...

Elizabeth and Zechariah had been married for a very long time, but they had no children and that made them both very sad. They longed for a baby but the years passed by and Elizabeth began to give up hope of ever becoming pregnant.

Then one day, something happened that changed all that. Zechariah was a priest, and he'd gone to work as usual in the Temple at Jerusalem. Other priests worked there too, but on this particular day it was

his turn to carry out a very important task. While everyone else was outside praying, Zechariah had to stay inside and make an offering to God. His task was to burn the sweet-smelling incense on the altar.

There he was, all alone, watching the smoke from the incense rising up to heaven, when he was startled by an angel, standing beside the altar. Zechariah was scared. What could this mean? An angel coming to him in the temple of God. Then the angel spoke. 'Zechariah, do not be afraid. God has asked me to bring you some excellent news. At last, your prayers have been answered. Elizabeth will have a baby son and you must name him John.'

Zechariah couldn't believe what he was hearing but there was more...

'John will grow up to be a great man,' said the angel. 'He will make you proud and happy. He will be a good man who will never touch wine nor alcohol, and right from his birth he will be filled with the goodness of the Lord. John has been chosen by God to prepare the people for the coming of the new King.'

It was too much for Zechariah. The angel seemed to be promising things that could never happen. 'How can I believe what you're telling me?' said Zechariah. 'My wife and I are old. How can we have a baby?'

'I am Gabriel, God's messenger,' said the angel. 'He sent me to tell you this excellent news. But listen. Because you've doubted His word, God will strike you dumb until after your son is born. You won't be able to speak until my words have come true.'

When Zechariah went home that evening he couldn't speak a word – he'd been struck dumb. Elizabeth was very worried. As fast as he could, Zechariah wrote down everything the angel had told him so that his wife would know what had happened, and what God was planning to do.

Stories

And that was how, when Mary came to visit, Elizabeth was six months pregnant, and she already knew all about God's promise to her young cousin.

Mary stayed with her cousins for three whole months, then she returned home to Nazareth, a few days before the birth of Elizabeth's son.

The time soon came for Elizabeth's baby son to be born. And when he was eight days old, the priests were invited to come to the house to dedicate the first-born son to God and give him his name, which is the custom under Jewish law. When the moment came for the baby to be named, the priests were going to name him Zechariah but Elizabeth said, 'No!' he was to be named John. 'But,' the priests argued, 'there is no one in your family called John. Surely, like all eldest sons, he'll be named after his father.'

Then Zechariah stood up. He still couldn't speak but he reached for his clay writing-tablet. 'His name is John,' he wrote, and immediately he got his voice back and began to talk. The first words he spoke were in praise of God, thanking him for the birth of his son.

Part 3

Meanwhile, back in Nazareth, Joseph, the town carpenter was very upset. He'd been looking forward to getting married, but when Mary returned from her visit to Elizabeth, she had some shocking news. She told him that she was going to have a baby. She'd tried to explain how God's messenger had appeared and told her that she had been chosen by God to be the mother of his Son. She, Mary, Joseph's wife-to-be, had been specially selected for that important task.

Joseph was a good man and he loved Mary, but how could he believe what she'd told him? He wanted to do what was right.

But what did that mean? It was a very strange story – angel-messengers and all that. There was only one thing he was sure about. Mary was pregnant. He'd seen her. She was beginning to put on weight. What could he do? People were starting to gossip. Nosy parkers! Why couldn't they mind their own business? The whole thing was making him miserable.

Finally, Joseph decided that the only thing to do was to break off the engagement. He went to bed feeling very sad. How on earth was he going to tell Mary that their wedding was off – that he couldn't marry her?

That night an angel appeared to him in a dream. 'Don't take any notice of the gossip,' said the angel. 'Mary's baby is the Son of God. She has been chosen by God to be the mother of Jesus. The name Jesus means "saviour". He'll save the people from their sins.'

Joseph woke feeling very happy. He knew exactly what to do. He would marry Mary and take good care of her and their baby.

Very soon after his dream, Joseph married Mary and she moved into his house in Nazareth. They were very happy. They had a lot to look forward to. They settled down to wait for the birth of their baby.

At that time, the country of Palestine was ruled by the Romans. And the Roman Emperor, Augustus, wanted to make sure that everyone paid their taxes. But he had a problem. He didn't know how many people lived in the Empire so he had no way of checking who had paid and who hadn't. Then Augustus had an idea. He gave an order for every adult male in the Empire to register at the town his family had come from. Once they had done that, he would have a list of all the people who should be paying taxes.

Joseph was a carpenter. He wasn't a rich man but he was descended from King

Stories ☆

David who had been born in the town of Bethlehem, far away in the south of Judaea. Because of the Emperor's order, Joseph would have to travel with Mary, through the hills, over stony roads, to register in Bethlehem. He was worried about how his young wife would manage on such a long journey. Their baby was due any day now.

'Don't worry,' said Mary. 'I'll pack some blankets and plenty of food and clothing. And I'd better take the baby clothes with me, just in case.'

Joseph loaded the bundles on to their donkey and they set off.

What a journey! Up hill and down dale – the heat of the day and the cold of the night. Oh, how Mary longed to have a proper meal and a good night's sleep!

Then, at last, they arrived in Bethlehem. At first they thought there must be a carnival. The town was packed. It was bursting at the seams. There were people and animals everywhere. It was like a zoo! And the noise! You wouldn't believe the noise. Donkeys were braying, goats were bleating, dogs were barking, people were shouting, children were crying, beggars were begging, and everywhere they went, families were rushing around, searching for places to stay.

Everywhere they looked there were signs saying 'FULL', 'NO VACANCIES' – there was no room at any of the inns.

It was already dark when Joseph called at the last inn. Mary was so tired, she could hardly walk.

'I'm sorry, we haven't got any rooms left,' said the innkeeper, 'and I see that your wife is heavily pregnant. How would you like to sleep in the stable with the animals? It's the best I can do.'

It'll be a bit smelly, thought Joseph, but at least, it'll be warm. 'Thanks,' he said, 'we'll take it.' And the innkeeper went off to find them some supper and to put down some more clean straw.

That very night the baby was born. Mary wrapped him snugly in the clothes she had made, and laid him in a manger. The Son of God was born in a stable. He was warm and safe, and Mary and Joseph could sleep in peace.

Part 4

But not everyone slept that night. On the quiet hills, outside the city, a group of shepherds were minding their sheep when suddenly, out of the darkness, an angel appeared, shining in a dazzle of light. The shepherds covered their faces in terror, then the angel spoke.

'Don't be afraid of me. I've got something wonderful to tell you. This is great news for you and all the world. A child has been born in Bethlehem. He's the promised King – the Saviour sent by God. Go and look for him. You'll find the baby lying in a manger.'

Then suddenly, the messenger-angel was surrounded by more angels, singing and praising God. The shepherds were amazed. They knew that something extraordinary must have happened.

When the angels had gone, the shepherds sat on the dark hillside and talked about what they had seen. 'We'd better go into Bethlehem,' they said. 'We should look for that baby and find out what's happened.'

So the shepherds went to Bethlehem, and found Mary and Joseph in the stable, with the baby lying in a manger, just as the angel had promised. When Mary heard their story she was overjoyed. She would always remember this night.

Mary and Joseph stayed on in Bethlehem, and when their baby was eight days old he was given the name Jesus. Afterwards, they took him to the Temple in Jerusalem for a special ceremony. In Jewish law, all first-born sons had to be dedicated to God.

Stories

But this baby was no ordinary child as Mary had come to realise. While they were still in Bethlehem a group of strangers arrived in Jerusalem and began asking questions. They were wise men from the east – astrologers and scientists – important men who studied the stars, and they had made an exciting discovery. A new star had appeared in the sky. It was large and very bright, and the wise men had been following it for many days.

'This star is a sign that a great king has been born,' they said. 'We must call upon King Herod. He's sure to know about the baby King.'

King Herod didn't know. No child had been born in his palace, but if the wise men were right, a new king had been born in Bethlehem. He didn't like that idea. He questioned the priests and the teachers who knew God's law.

'Is it true that when the Saviour comes he will be born in Bethlehem?'

'It's true,' they said. 'That's what is written in God's holy law.'

King Herod was a wicked man. He didn't want anyone else to be king so he arranged a secret meeting with the wise men. He'd thought of an evil plan.

'Go and search for the baby King in Bethlehem,' he said, 'and when you find him, come back and tell me where he is. Then I, too, can take him a gift.'

The wise men did as King Herod suggested. Travelling at night, when the stars shone like diamonds in the velvety darkness, they followed their special, pointed star until, at last, it came to rest over a house in Bethlehem.

'Can this be the place?' they said. 'It's neither a palace nor a rich man's house. Can this really be the home of the promised King?'

There was only one way to find out. They went inside and to their joy they found the baby Jesus snuggled in his mother's arms. At once, they knew that this was the King they'd been seeking.

Kneeling before the baby, they gave him their gifts – rare and expensive presents of gold, frankincense and myrrh.

They'd found the new-born King and now it was time to return home. But God, who knows everything, came to the wise men in a dream and warned them not to tell King Herod where Jesus could be found. They didn't go back to Jerusalem but travelled east by another road.

The wise men tricked King Herod but he wasn't going to give up. That night, an angel came to Joseph, in a dream, and told him of King Herod's plan. 'Get up, quickly, and take Mary and the baby to Egypt. King Herod will search for Jesus. If he finds him, he will kill him.'

Once again, Mary and Joseph had to make a long and difficult journey. In the dead of night, they loaded the donkey, and fled into Egypt. Like other refugees, they took only what they could carry. They had no idea how long they would have to stay in a foreign land.

When King Herod realised that the wise men had fooled him he flew into a frightening rage. He couldn't find the child who was born to be King, so he decided to kill every boy under the age of two. His cruelty was beyond belief and the people hated him.

It wasn't too long before King Herod died and, again, an angel came to Joseph in a dream and told him that it was safe to leave Egypt. But Mary and Joseph were afraid that the new King, who was Herod's son, might harm Jesus, so they didn't go back to Judaea. Instead, they went back to live in Nazareth. There they stayed and Jesus grew up. He was the Son of God but he never forgot to be a good son to his earthly parents, Mary and Joseph.

Stories ✪

All you need for Christmas

Finding a baby

Christmas plays are a good way of involving children in the Christmas activities. Fred Sedgwick has written a simple play for Key Stage 1 children to perform. Please note that you will need music of your own choice at a number of points during the play.

Characters

(The numbers given here refer to speaking parts. You can of course have as many angels/shepherds/lambs as you like!)

11 Children-narrators	An old man
4 Angels	A sad woman
4 Shepherds	2 Teachers (real ones, or children acting them)
Lambs	Bishop Nicholas/Father Christmas
3 Kings/Queens	A child's best friend

Overture – a single recorder plays a carol. Or piano, melody only.

CHILD 1 appears in front of the curtain, or at the front of an empty stage, dressed in his/her best.

Child 1   I was on my way to school today and I met some angels.

Enter ANGELS, some male, some female, all in white, but not necessarily traditional, robes.

1st Angel	Here is the news
2nd Angel	Glory to God in the highest
3rd Angel	And peace on earth
4th Angel	To all people of goodwill.
1st Angel	For unto us
2nd Angel	A child is born
3rd Angel	A son is given
1st Angel	And his name shall be called
2nd Angel	Wonderful! Counsellor!
1st Angel	The Mighty God!

☆ **Plays**

All you need for Christmas

3rd Angel	The Everlasting Father!
4th Angel	The Prince of Peace!

They proclaim all this to the audience, and wait, half of them on one side, half on the other.

CHILD 2 appears.

Child 2	I was on my way to school today and I met some angels and 20 shepherds.

SHEPHERDS arrive, perhaps from the back or side of the hall. Four children may be chosen to speak for the shepherds or children could be split into four groups, each of which speaks in unison.

1st Shepherd	Let's go to Bethlehem
2nd Shepherd	To see this thing
3rd Shepherd	That has happened
4th Shepherd	That the Lord has made known to us.

CHILD 3 appears.

Child 3	I was on my way to school today and I met some angels, 20 shepherds and some lambs.

SHEPHERDS show off a lamb or two.

CHILD 4 appears.

Child 4	I was on my way to school today and I met some angels, 20 shepherds, some lambs – and a donkey.

Loud donkey noise from off stage. Then the overture music, augmented with other instruments.

CHILD 5 appears.

Child 5	I was on my way to school today and I met some angels, 20 shepherds, some lambs, a donkey – and a few kings and queens.

Enter a few KINGS and QUEENS, bearing gifts.

1st King/Queen	I saw a star, and I'm looking for a baby.
2nd King/Queen	I've got a present, and I'm not telling you what it is until Christmas Day!
Child 5	Go on! Tell us!

Plays ✪

2nd King/Queen	No!
3rd King/Queen	I've got a present. And it's myrrh!
Child 2	Myrrh?!!
Child 3	*(Knowing look to audience)* And they asked us to do this myrrh often!
3rd King/Queen	Hold on a minute *(peeps)*. It's gold!
2nd King/Queen	*(Peeps)* Nah, it's frankincense.

KINGS/QUEENS sing an appropriate song.

CHILD 6 appears.

Child 6	I was on my way to school today and I met some angels, 20 shepherds, some lambs, a donkey, a few kings and queens – and an old man.
Old man	Hello there! I wrote a poem once. Would you like to hear it?

The OLD MAN insists.

Overture music as he speaks, this time more than single recorder augmented. Piano added?

Old man	I wrote a poem. A little kid chalked this poem on a dustbin lid.
The poem grew and it grew and grew – it was bigger than me and bigger than you!
It was bigger than Miss as it unfurled, it was bigger than everything, even the world.
It was bigger than the sea and the sky above, it was bigger than the universe...

Long pause.

	Its name was love.
Child 7	I was on my way to school today and I met some angels, 20 shepherds, some lambs, a few kings and queens, an old man – and a sad woman.
Sad woman	Hello! Do you want to hear my song?

Choose an appropriate song – try Ralph McTell's 'Streets of London' if you can't think of any other.

Plays

Sad woman	I'm not sure what's going on here, but I want to see it.
Child 7	Just wait a moment longer. It's for you as much as anyone else.
Child 8	I was on my way to school today and I met some angels, 20 shepherds, some lambs, a few kings and queens, an old man, a sad woman – and my teacher!

The FIRST TEACHER arrives on scene. This could be the actual teacher or a child impersonating him or her.

1st Teacher	There was a family. A sad family. The mother had been dead many, many years.

Enter 2nd TEACHER (a real one, or a child).

2nd Teacher	The father was out of work, and they had little food.
1st Teacher	And he had three daughters, who were hungry, and thirsty, and tired of the hard work they had to do to get what food they had – scraps of stale bread, old vegetables, bony, fatty meat.
2nd Teacher	One night, the food ran out completely.
1st Teacher	The cupboard was more bare than Mother Hubbard's, and they had nothing at all to eat.
2nd Teacher	No beans, no spuds
1st Teacher	No chicken, no beef.
2nd Teacher	No fruit, no veg
1st Teacher	No root, no leaf.
2nd Teacher	Nothing for the cow, not even cuds
1st Teacher	No soup, or steak and kidney puds.
2nd Teacher	Nothing to put between their lips
1st Teacher	No pizza, curry, fish and chips!
2nd Teacher	Meanwhile, Bishop Nicholas, a very important man in the nearby city, heard about them.
Child 1	Bishop Nicholas?
Child 2	Yes, you know, Santa Claus.
Child 3	Yes! Father Christmas!
2nd Teacher	And he thought, why should anyone be so poor they can't get enough to eat?

Plays ✪

☆Finding a baby

Sad woman	Good point.
1st Teacher	And…

Pause.

2nd Teacher	Before he knew what he was doing
1st Teacher	He'd filled a sack with toys
2nd Teacher	And turkey and bread and wine
1st Teacher	And he found the poor man's house
2nd Teacher	Under the Big Star sign…
1st Teacher	And…
2nd Teacher	Tipped it down the poor man's chimney!

CAST cheers as BISHOP NICHOLAS/FATHER CHRISTMAS comes on and spills a sack of goodies onto the stage.

All sing a carol such as 'Good King Wenceslas'.

1st Teacher	I met a child, and she was looking for a baby.
Child 9	I was on my way to school today and I met some angels, 20 shepherds, some lambs, a few kings and queens, an old man, a sad woman, my teachers – and my best friend.
Best friend	My friend is looking for a baby – and so am I!
Child 10	And they all sat down.

They sit down.

Child 11	And there were Mary and Joseph and Jesus.

The traditional Nativity scene is suddenly exposed behind the children.

Child 1	Look! Some angels, 20 shepherds, some lambs, a few kings and queens, an old man, a sad woman, my teachers and my best friend.
Child 2	And Father Christmas!
Child 3	And they've found a baby!

Final carol, with as big an instrumentation and choir as possible, to contrast with the bare opening of one recorder or melody piano.

✪ **Plays**

Mary of Ephesus

This play for Key Stage 2 children by Fred Sedgwick requires singers and musicians as well as the cast. The musicians and singers can perform whatever they think is appropriate. The play is flexible – there is room for creative development for both teachers and children. If any of it is inappropriate to your school, cut it out.

NOTE for programmes, etc.

Muslims living in western Turkey believe that Mary lived there in the latter part of her life. Indeed, visitors to Ephesus can visit the house in which she died. This play uses that tradition, and the first two chapters of St Luke's Gospel.

NOTE for producers

Use this play flexibly, but keep Mary at the centre. The scenery should be as simple as possible – bits and pieces that'll serve all the scenes, eg. hay bales, stools, benches. There should be as little movement of scenery and props as you can get away with.

Preparation

Children can be taught these passages from St Luke's Gospel, 1: 26–35, 1: 46–55, 2: 1–19, and 15: 3–7. Paintings of scenes from these stories could be displayed.

Characters (in order of appearance)

3 old women	3 angels
1 man	Father Christmas
Young Mary	Father Christmas's assistant
Mary's friends (3 or more)	Joseph
Gabriel	Kings
4 shepherds	

Plays ✪

Scene One: Ephesus, AD 50

THREE WOMEN and a MAN on stage. The WOMEN are getting on in years.

The FIRST WOMAN comes to the front of the stage and speaks to the audience. The other two WOMEN and the MAN listen, sitting upstage

1st Woman	It was a long, long time ago. The couple had been pushed about, road to road, town to town, pillar to post…
2nd Woman	*(Joining the WOMAN and interrupting)* Pillar to post! You try living in an occupied country, you'll know what she means –
	She looks, challengingly, at the audience
3rd Woman	*(Joining the others)* Go here, go there, go here, get on the end of a queue and find it's the wrong one, have you filled this form in, there's a census this year...
Man	*(Joining the others)* You might as well be in the 21st century, shoved from here to there, there to here, ship to ship, camp to camp!
1st Woman	*(Interrupting, but patiently – this is, after all, her story. She has great dignity)* These two had been pushed about…
3rd Woman	*(Interrupting)* The town was dark as a camp at midnight.
	If possible the lights slowly begin to darken from now until the end of the scene
	There were a few stars. A few candles burning in upper rooms. A few meals being eaten, bread and wine…
2nd Woman	*(Dreamily)* Bread and wine…
Man	And a few more with stale bread and water…
3rd Woman	And yet more with nothing at all, and beggars lying hungry under the stars…
Man	Unable to rejoice.
1st Woman	*(Patiently taking up the story again)* Nothing out of the ordinary. And then this couple came…
3rd Woman	*(Interrupting)* She was like a pear, walking, more tired than you are when you've walked to the shops and back again, forgotten something, gone back, come back...
1st Woman	Tired isn't the word…

❉ **Plays**

She looks, suddenly, at the audience. By now, the stage is nearly dark, except for a light on the WOMAN, some of which spreads to the others

Man   I felt as though something I'd been waiting for was about to happen.

2nd Woman   *(To the audience)* Do you want to hear about it?

1st Woman   *(Quietly)* Do you want to hear my story?

Perhaps the audience could be cajoled into a positive response

2nd Woman   And while you do, bear in mind what they say in the synagogue…

3rd Woman   Behold, a virgin shall conceive, and bear a son, and shall call his name, Emmanuel, 'God with us'…

2nd Woman   You won't understand any of it, unless you remember that.

3rd Woman   Emmanuel…

1st Woman   God with us.

2nd Woman   This is all about good news…

3rd Woman   And that is it.

The lights on the stage go up again. The WOMEN and the MAN go to the sides of the stage, and watch intently during the next scene. They are less well lit

Scene Two: Nazareth, 1 BC

Normal light

MARY is playing with friends – let the children decide. Perhaps they are dancing, skipping, tossing a ball about

2nd Woman   *(From the side of the stage)* She was a nice kid, full of life and fun…

*Let the children (preferably) write dialogue here –
What do you say to your friends when you're playing? What clapping/singing/skipping games do you use?*

Or, failing that, use the following, or any variation of it

My name is little Lizzie,
I'm in a fearful tizzy,
when in he comes,
with his big red thumbs,
and this is what he said:

Plays ✪

© **pfp** publishing limited 2002 ISBN 1 874050 59 7 May be photocopied for use only within the purchasing institution **pfp**, 61 Gray's Inn Road, London WC1X 8TH **pfp**

Will you come to the dance, love (dance with me),
will you meet my mum, love (and have some tea)?

Will you love me, Lizzie, till the day I die –
Oh! marry me, Lizzie or – I – will – cry…

Most children will be able to work out clapping or skipping to this. Ends with all falling over, and great laughter

1st Woman   *Moving out of her partial darkness* Then a stranger appears, and changes more than one life with a single word.

Enter GABRIEL, imperious and statusque

He is dressed in – let the children decide. But if he is in all white, he has no wings or robes. Evening gear? Something very flashy?

The cast could (preferably) write the Gabriel/Mary dialogue, having read Luke and looked at pictures of the Annunciation. Otherwise, use the following

Gabriel   Be glad, you are highly favoured and the Lord is with you…

Mary   *(Turns her back on GABRIEL, greatly troubled. To the audience)* I'm not special. Or highly favoured, whatever that may mean. I love the Lord. And I know He's with me. But – I want to go on playing. *(Turns to GABRIEL)* Sir…

GABRIEL remains imperious, statuesque

Mary's 1st friend   Leave her alone, Sir…

Mary's 2nd friend   We keep ourselves to ourselves – er, *(cheekily)* mate!

And they go on playing, keeping a wary eye on GABRIEL. The playing goes on during the following dialogue

Gabriel   Mary, do not be afraid…

1st Woman   *(Pleadingly, insistently, from the side)* Listen, love!

Gabriel   You have won God's favour.

1st Woman   Darling lady, listen!

Gabriel   You will have a Son.

Playing freezes

And His name will be Jesus *(Pause)*

And He will be great *(Pause)*

Plays

And He will be the Son of the Most High. *(Pause)*

The Lord God will give Him the throne of His ancestor David *(Pause)*

And His reign will never, never end.

Long pause. MARY rises and goes towards GABRIEL very slowly

Mary   How can that be, since I've never known a man?

Gabriel   The Holy Spirit will come upon you *(Pause)*

and the power of the Most High will cover you with its shadow. *(Pause)*

The child will be the Son, not of a man, *(Pause)* but of God.

MARY'S FRIENDS leave one by one, looking back at MARY who is in centre stage, on her own. As this happens, the lights go down slowly. MARY looks across at the FIRST WOMAN, and their eyes meet

They could share a small shrug or a smile or even run to each other and hug

3rd Woman   *(To the audience)* Remember what I said? A virgin shall conceive, and bear a son, and shall call his name 'God with us'…

1st Woman   You must ponder these things in your heart, my love.

Song – a carol about Mary

Everyone leaves the stage during this song except MARY

Darkness, under cover of which MARY leaves

Scene Three: Bethlehem, 1 BC

Lights up

FOUR SHEPHERDS – JAMES, DANIEL, PETER and JOHN – run on to stage. THIRD WOMAN and MAN are at the side. JOHN is always last, a beat behind the others in everything. He is also the smallest of the group, by as much as possible. Make the others very tall. They need not, of course, be boys. Change names as appropriate. It might be useful to use the children's real names for these parts. JOHN should aim at bringing out the 'aahhhs!' from the audience. You can even make the shepherd scenes into pantomime

3rd Woman   There were shepherds in the fields…

Man   Watching over their sheep…

3rd Woman   By night.

James	It's your fault, Daniel. You lost him!
Daniel	I wasn't supposed to be looking after the new lamb, Peter was!
Peter	It's all John's fault

JOHN makes a 'Who, me?' face. Very indignant

James	You're not pulling the wool over my eyes! It was Daniel's responsibility.
Daniel	*(Squaring up)* I'll flay you alive…
Peter	Cut it out, let's find this lamb.

They nearly come to blows, and the first three go out quarrelling in dumbshow. JOHN looks at the audience, on his own on the big stage. Puckers his face as if he is going to cry. He resists for as long as possible. The actor playing JOHN might look around for his parents

John	I want my Mummy!/Daddy!

Cries

Scene Four

Lights low

Mary lit higher than the rest. She also might be on a slightly higher level

MARY and FRIENDS in a circle. The FIRST WOMAN and SECOND and THIRD WOMAN join in. Also, the MAN. They could persuade the audience to join in on the repeated line. Holding it up on a board will help if you want them to do so

Mary	My soul magnifies the Lord. My spirit rejoices in God my Saviour, because He's looked on this lowly lady.
Friends	My soul magnifies the Lord.
Mary	From today, all generations will call me blessed, for the Almighty has done great things for me, Holy is His name.
Friends	My soul magnifies the Lord.
Mary	His mercy reaches everyone who fears Him. He has shown the strength of His arm. He has scattered the proud, the show-offs, the bigheads.
Friends	My soul magnifies the Lord.

Plays

Mary	He has pulled down princes, put high the lowest of the low, He has filled the hungry, sent the rich away. He has come to help Israel, his servant...
Friends	My soul magnifies the Lord.
Mary	...according to those promises made to Abraham and his descendants.
Friends	My soul magnifies the Lord.
All *(including audience)*	My soul magnifies the Lord. My soul magnifies the Lord. My soul magnifies the Lord.

Over this repetition comes a carol about Mary

Scene Five

Lights up

The FOUR SHEPHERDS enter, still quarrelling, JOHN last

James	If we don't find that lamb, we're for it. He'll fleece us!
Peter	I feel quite queasy thinking about it.
Daniel	I felt queasy before I thought about it!
James	He'll have our guts for garters…
Daniel	Our eyeballs for marbles…
James	The heels of our feet for boxing gloves…
Daniel	Our brains for cauli…
Peter	Oh shut up! and let's find that lamb! I'll murder that John one day.
John	Me? Why does everyone blame me?
James	*(Ignoring JOHN)* He's right! Let's look everywhere.

Manic activity. They look under, over, round, beneath, above, through things. They stare into the wings, look directly upwards

Then, suddenly inspired at the same moment (except, of course, for JOHN, who is a second or two behind the others) they start looking among the audience, picking up bags, looking under coats, etc. As much mayhem as possible to be allowed here, as long as it can be stopped suddenly for the following

(Perhaps schools may feel all this is inappropriate. If so, cut it, right up to the end of the scene.)

Plays ✪

John	(Top of his voice, to the teacher in charge, or the pianist, or the headteacher)
	Miss!/Sir!? Can I go home now? I'm scared.
The adult	No, John, of course not. Just find that lamb.
	JOHN, now back on stage, gazes sorrowfully at the audience. Puckers hugely. Bursts into tears
James	Now back on stage as well – the others follow – grabs JOHN's hand I wish I'd never been a shepherd. I wish I'd been an angel, like my sister Kate.
	Or, if he has a sister/angel, her real name
	Does a great angel imitation, arms as wings, pious expression. Holds this until 'boss people about' [below], when he joins in the bossing.
Daniel	Comes downstage I'd've made a great king. I kept telling them.
	With a look to the teacher-in-charge, or the headteacher
	Remember King David. He was a shepherd. A shepherd-boy, even! Just watch me kneel.
	He does so, very slowly, with great dignity, to the audience, maybe milking a round of applause. Stands up suddenly.
	Just see me wear a crown.
	He places a crown on his head, slowly in great dumbshow. Or maybe he suddenly produces a paper crown from somewhere.
	And watch me (pause)… boss people about!
	Of course, here he (and JAMES) can boss the head, his parents, the pianist, whoever he likes. Let him make his own lines up. Then he and JAMES go upstage.
Peter	I was set for higher things, as well.
	Confidentially, to the audience, in huge stage whisper
	I'm the understudy for Joseph!
	He mimes being a good protective husband, maybe with JOHN as Mary.
John	(Through his tears) They wanted me to be a sheep, but I stood up for myself.
	Draws himself up to his full height
	They sigh

● **Plays**

Peter	Well, the lamb isn't here.
James	*(Pointing)* It wasn't there.
Daniel	*(Pointing)* Or there.
James	*(Pointing)* Or over there. Come on, let's go. He'll have our guts for garters…
Daniel	Our eyeballs for marbles…
James	The heels of our feet for boxing gloves…
Daniel	Our brains for cauli…
Peter	Oh shut up!

They each, cheekily, check under a teacher's chair, or the chair of governors' chair. They go, perhaps, for their parents' chairs. They leave, JOHN falling over again.

John	*(Getting up)* Please can I go home?
Headteacher	*(From the audience)* No.

Scene Six

Three angels. ANGEL 3 is different from the others, trendy, long-haired, hippy, possibly. Though each cast can decide how she/he is different. Maybe she/he isn't different at all… But it would be best if the angels were a mix of sexes, and, if possible, races.

They are getting ready for a performance. Perhaps they are setting up music stands. If one is a recorder player, she/he might accompany the hymn that ends this scene.

Angel 1	This is going to terrify those shepherds looking for that lamb.
Angel 2	Yes. Still. Never mind.

As if practising, making sure she/he has learned it by heart, emphasising the important words

For unto us a child is born, unto us a Son is given, and His name shall be called Wonderful, Counsellor, the Mighty God, the Prince of Peace…

Angel 1	Poor shepherds! They're only mortals! They're not like us. It's hard to imagine what this'll do to them.
Angel 2	Have you got the music? This is our best gig so far. I do think you ought to practise.

Again, as if practising, same emphases as before

Plays ✪

| | For unto us a child is born, unto us a Son is given, and His name shall be called… |
| Angel 3 | Yup. Good gig. That's pukka. Well, better than the Harvest Festival. |

Or some other recent school event that had music

| Angel 1 | OK Shepherds, you've got it coming. Brace yourselves. Hold on to your crooks. |
| Angel 3 | Let's shake this hit man. Let's kick it from the top. |

Or preferably, replace this with current slang terms gleaned from the children

| Angel 2 | Have we really practised enough? |

Again, as if practising

| | For unto us a child is born, unto us a son is given, and his name shall be called Wonderful… |
| Angel 3 | *(Interrupts)* Ah – one, ah – two, ah – one, two, three, four… |

'Hark the Herald Angels Sing' is sung, first verse just the angels, the rest with whole audience, very traditionally. ANGELS encourage the audience to sing – even, if you dare, picking on prominent non-singers in the audience.

As the second verse of the hymn ends, the shepherds enter, the lost lamb forgotten in their terror. They look at the angels (who are upstage) speechlessly, mouths ridiculously open, expressing their fear to the audience. They step around the angels (downstage) on tiptoe and in slow motion, as if trying to escape without being noticed. The first three are in step. JOHN, of course, is out of step, and always at the back.

| Angel 1 | *(Once there is silence again, and rather suddenly, directly at JOHN)* **Don't worry!** |

JOHN leaps back, falls on his bottom.

| Angel 2 | *(Picking him up, and cuddling him, sitting with him on a bench, perhaps)* **Fear not! Chin up!** |
| Angel 3 | Cool it man! |

Ruffles JOHN's hair

SHEPHERDS gibber with fear

| Angel 1 | We bring you tidings – |

Arms round DANIEL's and PETER's necks

Plays

All you need for Christmas

Angel 2	Of great joy.

Shaking JAMES's hand thoroughly

Angel 3	Lighten up brothers and sisters. Especially *(To JOHN)* little guys.

JOHN, fear momentarily forgotten, looks daggers at him

Angel 1	For everybody.

Still especially with DANIEL and PETER

Angel 2	The whole world.

Hugging JAMES

Angel 3	Even *(with a mock-ferocious glare at JOHN)* shepherds.

The shepherds glance warily at each other. Then the angels leave the shepherds to drop where they are, and come downstage. They say the following very importantly, possibly beginning like a news broadcast

Angel 1	*(Loud)* Today in David's town
Angel 2	*(Very loud)* A Saviour has been born
Angel 3	*(Louder still)* And He is Christ the Lord!

'Hark the Herald Angels Sing' third verse.

ANGELS exhort the audience to sing. When the hymn ends, they leave.

Then, having forgotten something, ANGEL 2 reappears.

Angel 2	*(Out of breath)* Oh! Sorry!

Takes time to get his/her breath back. Waves everyone to silence, if necessary

Oh dear!

Eventually, and very stately

For unto us a child is born, unto us a son is given, and His name shall be called Wonderful…

Angel 1	*(Reappears)* Counsellor, the Mighty God,
Angel 3	*(Reappears and says very slowly and loudly: this is important!)* the Prince of Peace…

Pause

They leave, chucking JOHN under the chin, ruffling his hair, etc.

Plays ✪

Scene Seven

The SHEPHERDS are left in stunned silence.

James	That was good news.
Daniel	Certainly was!
Peter	It reminded me of that thing they say in the synagogue, you know, how does it go…?
Daniel	He shall feed his flock like a shepherd
Peter	He shall gather the lambs with his arm
Daniel	and carry them in his arms
Peter	and gently lead those that are with young.
Daniel	I feel better already.
James	I'm all warm inside.
Daniel	I feel like I've been filled with good things…
Peter	I know! I know! And the rich have been sent away empty!
James	I feel peace, and goodwill to all people.
Daniel	Yeah!
James	Great!
Peter	Wow-ee!

They beam at each other. Hug each other. Sixties peace behaviour. Then, freeze. As long as you can bear it.

James	But what about our lamb?

Expressions change comically. Long pause. They burst into tears. All at the same time.

Except JOHN, who is a moment late. They go. Lights down.

Scene Eight

Lights up.

The traditional nativity tableau: MARY, JOSEPH, baby. The SHEPHERDS enter. All kneel

'Once in Royal David's City', first three verses, the first verse a solo, in the traditional manner

Then enter FATHER CHRISTMAS and ASSISTANT. The family stay dignified and quiet during the rest of this, which mainly involves the shepherds

Plays

Father Christmas	Today is Christmas Day, if you but knew it. One day it'll be a day for chimneys and reindeer and eating too much.
Assistant	One day it'll be a day for presents and turkey and Christmas crackers.
Father Christmas	One day it'll be a day for Aunts and Uncles and cousins to stay and drink all the sherry.
Assistant	One day it'll be a day for the Queen's Christmas broadcast, the service of nine lessons and carols, icing and marzipan…
Father Christmas	One day it'll be a day for seeing Mummy kissing Santa Claus, and for you kissing your best-looking cousin under the mistletoe.
Assistant	But…
Father Christmas	today it's a day for…
Whole cast	Glory to God in the highest, and on earth, peace to all people.
Father Christmas	And…

(Long significant pause, looks at JOHN)

for finding lost lambs! For what shepherd, having one hundred sheep, and losing one…

Assistant	doesn't leave the ninety-nine in the desert, and go in search…
Father Christmas	of the one that's lost?

During this dialogue (above) he produces the lamb from backstage. He gives it to JOHN. Who hugs it and places it next to the cradle.

'We Wish You a Merry Christmas', or some other song is sung, during which the Kings arrive, from various corners of the hall, with gifts

ALL freeze

Scene Nine: Ephesus, AD 50

The lights go up on the WOMEN and the MAN, who are around the sides of the stage.

They look at the scene. Move towards it

28

1st Woman	That was how it was…
3rd Woman	You remember it best, don't you…
1st Woman	Of course I do. That was my story. That was when we were young, a moment or two ago.
Man	I felt, I feel – I can go in peace now.

MARY comes over. Puts the baby in the FIRST WOMAN's arms. Stays with her.

Man	It was as though I'd seen salvation…
Mary	I pondered and pondered all these things in my heart. And through all the tinsel, there it was still.
2nd Woman	There was what?
Mary	My soul magnifying the Lord.
1st Woman	And…
Mary	And there was this baby…
Man	A light to enlighten everyone, Jew, non-Jew, Greek, black, white, Asian, man, woman…
2nd Woman	Rich and poor, kings and beggars…
3rd Woman	In palaces and camps, on the sea, in the air…
Man	Salvation for all people…
2nd Woman	Emmanuel. God with us.
1st Woman	The light for everyone…

She sighs. Then smiles through her sighs. FIRST WOMAN and MARY hug.

A solo recorder plays 'Mary, Mary' or some other carol with Mary at the centre.

CURTAIN.

Plays

What's on tonight, dear?

This Christmas play has been written by David Day for upper Key Stage 2 children to perform, although children in lower Key Stage 2 could participate in some of the sketches and children of all ages will enjoy watching it.

NOTES for producers

The Christmas story is, in essence, a collage of different elements. This play attempts to link them through the idea of programmes on different television channels. Fred and Bertha are the two characters responsible for creating that linkage, and they are meant to be 'larger than life'.

Appearance

Fred – trousers, string vest, slippers, unshaven and equipped with his essential accessory, a can of drink. Bertha – floral dress, slippers, hair in curlers, over-the-top lipstick. Other characters – whatever seems appropriate.

Stage set

The play is set in Fred and Bertha's living room. There are two chairs towards the front at one side of the stage, with a TV diagonally opposite. Sketches from the Christmas story are acted out in the space in between, as if they were programmes on the TV.

Characters (in order of appearance)

Fred (entire play)
Bertha (entire play)
Mary (sketches 1, 4, 5 and 7)
Angel (sketches 1 and 6)
Balthazar (sketches 2, 3 and 7)
Astronomer (sketches 2 and 3)
Servant (sketch 2)
Caspar (sketches 2, 3 and 7)
Melchior (sketches 2, 3, and 7)
Herod (sketch 3)
2 Guards (sketch 3)
Slave (sketch 3)

2 Ministers (sketch 3)
Herod's servant (sketch 3)
Joseph (sketches 4, 5 and 7)
3 Travellers (sketch 4)
Fred and Bertha's son (end of sketch 4 onwards)
Bethlehem crowd (sketch 5)
Innkeeper 1 (sketch 5)
Innkeeper 2 (sketches 5 and 7)
5 Shepherds(sketches 6 and 7)
Reporter (sketch 7)

Plays ✪

pfp

30

Scene One

Enter FRED and BERTHA. FRED carries a can of drink and rubs his stomach

Fred	That was smashing grub, love – all those lovely spuds.
Bertha	I don't know, Fred. All you think about is your stomach. They say the way to a man's heart is through his stomach and I reckon they're right.
Fred	And it's true, my lovely. Anyway – you can't talk – you scoffed yours quickly enough. Who finished off the apple pie, then? Come on, Bertha – own up!
Bertha	Let's drop the subject, shall we? It's rather boring. Honestly, if a girl can't enjoy a second helping every now and again…
Fred	Girl? Some girl!
Bertha	What about the washing up, Fred? You do that while I find my knitting. Now then, where did I leave it? Was it in here or did I leave it in the bathroom? *(Starts a search)*
Fred	Washing up? We'll do that later, love. *(Stretches)* What I fancy now is a nice spot of telly watching…
Bertha	By way of a change! *(Aside)* Honestly – he does nothing else!
Fred	What's on tonight, dear?
Bertha	How should I know? The TV guide is over there. *(Points to TV guide on FRED's chair)* Use your eyes. I mean, what's the point of having it if you can't be bothered to read it? You expect me to do everything around here. Now, where is that knitting?
Fred	Now then… *(Picks up TV guide)* Let's get ourselves nice and comfy… *(Sits)* Yeeeeeeeeaaaaaaaarrrrrrgggggghhhh!!!!! *(Springs up)* This wouldn't be your knitting, would it? In my chair? Cor, stone the crows! *(Rubs bottom vigorously)*
Bertha	Ah – thank you, Fred. So that's where those needles were all the time… Something wrong, dear?
Fred	Wrong? Wrong? Oh no – nothing's wrong at all. I've just been savaged to death by a vicious pair of knitting needles and I probably need urgent medical attention but, no – nothing's wrong at all. Please don't spare a thought for me.

Plays

Bertha	That's alright, then. *(Sits)* That's nice. Now then, what's the next stitch… *(BERTHA knits on and off for the rest of the play)* What's on the TV, Fred?
Fred	Well… Not much as far as I can see. *Eastenders*, of course… and *Brookside*. The rest is just Christmas stuff.
Bertha	What do you mean by Christmas stuff?
Fred	Oh, you know – twits standing around in the snow singing and that. I mean, you've got to be stupid to want to get cold like that, I reckon! Why can't there be something good on?
Bertha	Because it *is* Christmas, Fred. Not everyone's as miserable as you. Let's see what's on the BBC. Ever so educational, the BBC is.
Fred	*(Aside)* That's what's wrong with me, then!
Bertha	'Spect so. Yeah, there's more Christmas programmes here… *(Checks TV guide)*
Fred	Boring!
Bertha	Well, I like some of it. Oh, look – it says *The Angel Appears to Mary*. Let's watch that, shall we?
Fred	*(Rises and switches channels)* Doesn't look exactly exciting, does it?
Bertha	Oh, stop belly-aching, Fred! You're always moaning.
Fred	Sorry, love. *(Mock excitement)* Oh, golly… this looks exciting… rather… wow! *(BERTHA looks at him, annoyed. FRED mutters)* Never mind, Fred… Pour yourself another drink, Fred… Shut up, Fred… *(Sits)*
Bertha	Shhh! It's starting…
Fred	*(Heavy sarcasm)* Yes. That would be because I switched it on.

Sketch 1 – Mary's bedroom

Enter MARY, looking ready for bed. Goes to centre stage and stretches, but there is a call of 'Mary' from off-stage and she goes to the side and talks as if holding a conversation

Mary	Yes, Mum? Yes, I'm off to bed now. It's going to be a long day tomorrow. Pardon? Yes, Mum, I fed the donkey. Sorry? Yes, I tidied up outside. Yes, and I filled the urn. No – I didn't. Yes. Yes, I did. OK, I'll do that. No. No, I won't. Yes. Yes, I will… Goodnight,

Plays ✪

☆What's on tonight, dear?

	Mum. *(Moves to centre stage)* Bed. Wonderful. I could sleep for a hundred years. Just do my hair a moment. *(Brushes)* Not bad. I ought to wash it but tomorrow will have to do. I'm just too tired. Bed… Ah, bed… *(Lies down and falls asleep)*
Fred	No Slumberland in those days, you know. Horde of fleas in that straw, probably.
Bertha	A bit hard, I would have thought. Isn't she lovely…
Fred	Who, her? OK, I suppose. Is that it?
Bertha	Alright, it's not very exciting at present, I grant you!
Fred	I'm not going to sit and listen to a bird snoring away all evening. I listen to you all night and that's enough!
	Enter ANGEL
Bertha	Oooo, look. It's an angel.
Fred	How would you know? You ever seen one?
Bertha	No, but… Well, it's obvious, isn't it? I mean, look at those great big wings.
Fred	I could put wings on. It wouldn't make me an angel!
Angel	Mary… Mary… *(Pause)* Mary. Wake up, Mary.
Fred	It's no use, mate – she won't hear you.
Angel	Mary, wake up and listen to me. Mary, wake up.
Mary	What? Who's making all that din? Can't I sleep in peace?
Angel	Mary, I want you to wake up. Wake up now, please.
Mary	What is it, Mum? What's going on? What… *(Sees ANGEL and becomes very afraid)* Who are you?
Angel	It's alright, Mary. I'm…
Mary	What are you doing in my room? Get out! Mum!
Angel	Mary, just listen to me.
Mary	Get out! Get out! Now! Mum!
Angel	I mean you no harm, Mary.
Mary	Who are you? You've no right to be in my room. You frightened the living daylights out of me… How do you know my name?
Angel	God knows everything and everyone, Mary.
Mary	So you're God, are you? You expect me to fall for that? I'm not daft, you know!

✪ **Plays**

Angel	God sent me to talk to you, Mary. He told me where to find you.
Mary	Oh yeah, right! So why didn't you come and knock on the door, then?
Angel	Would you have let me in?
Mary	'Course not. Mum taught me never to open the door to strangers.
Angel	Well, then, you see my problem. So, will you talk to me?
Mary	*(Visibly calming)* You didn't half give me a fright.
Angel	Obviously, and I'm sorry. My name is Gabriel, by the way. I'm an angel.
Mary	You're a what?
Angel	An angel. I'm one of God's messengers.
Mary	You mean… this connection with God is real? You really expect me to go along with that?
Angel	I'm afraid so. Mary – your door is locked. There is no window here I could have climbed through. I have sort of 'appeared'. Please try to believe that I'm an angel. God has chosen you from all the people in this country to carry out a special task.
Mary	This is becoming really serious. You wouldn't be saying something like that if it wasn't true. What… What is this special job?
Angel	Mary, prepare yourself for this, because it's going to take your breath away…
Mary	Yes… well… go on – I'm ready.
Angel	God has chosen you from all the young women in the country.
Mary	Oh my goodness…
Angel	He has been looking for someone who has led a life free from sin, and that means in thoughts as well as actions.
Mary	Well, yes, I have tried to follow God's laws, but…
Angel	I can't prepare you for this. I think I'll just tell you straight. God has selected you to be the mother of his son, Mary.
Mary	Wha…?
Angel	Don't argue, Mary, and don't ask questions. Just listen. Now, then, can I continue? *(MARY nods)* You are going to

Plays ✪

☆What's on tonight, dear?

	have a baby and…
Mary	I most certainly am not. I'm not pregnant. I'm not married and I have followed the law. It's impossible. I'm engaged to Joseph, but there's no baby, I promise you!
Angel	Nothing is impossible to God, Mary. You know that.
Mary	*(In a small voice)* This isn't some kind of joke?
Angel	Oh, no. This is no joke. This is the real thing and, before you ask, you're not dreaming.
Mary	Yes, I was going to ask that. *(Small smile)* I can't take this in. I'm going to have a baby?
Angel	Yes.
Mary	And the father will be God?
Angel	Yes.
Mary	And God knows I'm a fairly good person?
Angel	Yes.
Mary	I sort of understand but then – I don't. I'm… sort of… stunned. But… if it's what God wants, then who am I to say no?
Angel	It's a real honour, Mary. You will have a son. You should call him Jesus.
Mary	Jesus. *(Kneels)* I am God's servant. I will do what he wants me to do. Even so, I can't take it in…
Angel	Nobody expects you to, Mary. Go back to sleep, now, before we wake the household. Sleep. God is with you.
	MARY sleeps for a moment
	Exit ANGEL and MARY
Fred	Let's try another channel now, love. I want a programme with a bit of guts.
Bertha	*(Looking at the TV guide)* It says here that all this took place in Nazareth.
Fred	Haven't they got a football team?
Bertha	It says '…the angel appeared also to Joseph' – that must be the young man she said she was engaged to – 'and told him of God's plans. Joseph was a very honest man and accepted the angel's message. He married

Plays

Fred	Mary and settled down to await the birth of the child.' That's it, then. End of story. I'm going to try another channel even if you don't fancy it. *(Gets up and walks over to TV to change channels)* Hey. That's better – look at all those posh robes.
Bertha	*(As FRED returns to his chair)* You're a very selfish man, Fred. I liked that nice Mary's angel programme. Well, if we have to watch it, you might read out what it says.
Fred	Eh? Oh… it says here… *The Great Palace of King Balthazar*. Action – here we come!

Sketch 2 – The Great Palace of King Balthazar

Enter BALTHAZAR and ASTRONOMER

Balthazar	So. What you're trying to tell me is that a new king is about to be born.
Astronomer	Yes, Sire. Without a doubt, it will be very soon now. The stars are all in position and the signs…
Balthazar	Yes, yes, you told me. It's rather more complicated than you realise.
Astronomer	I am only doing my duty, Sire. You know what must be done, not I.
Balthazar	True, Astronomer, true. Thank you for your information. I don't yet know if it is good or bad news.

Enter SERVANT

Servant	Their Majesties, King Caspar and King Melchior.

Enter CASPAR and MELCHIOR

Balthazar	Friends! Friends, how glad I am to see you!
Caspar	And we, you, Balthazar, old fellow. We came as soon as we received your warning.
Melchior	Are you absolutely sure that the time has come?
Balthazar	Well, this is the man to ask. Come now, Astronomer Royal. What is your answer?
Astronomer	Sires… I… You see…
Melchior	Out with it, man!
Caspar	Patience. He has to address three kings all at the same time. It's enough to shake the confidence of anyone,

Plays ✪

© **pfp** publishing limited 2002 ISBN 1 874050 59 7 May be photocopied for use only within the purchasing institution **pfp**, 61 Gray's Inn Road, London WC1X 8TH

36

	especially looking at the frown on your face, Melchior, old fruit!
Astronomer	Sires, there is no doubt that a great king will be born, and it will be quite soon. But I cannot tell you where, or who the parents are…
Melchior	What use is that? We don't know where, who or when. This is a waste of time. Pah!
Astronomer	There is, however, Sires, the star.
All	The star?
Melchior	What star?
Balthazar	That one. *(Points through a window)* It appears that all we have to do is follow it.
Caspar	Yes, maybe, but for how far, and will it wait for us while we rest?
Melchior	I don't like it. It smells of magic to me. *I'm* a king and people don't need a star to find me.
Balthazar	Well, I'm for following the star and finding this so-called king.
Caspar	Yes, but it might take time.
Melchior	Certainly, a king who has his own star is likely to be very powerful. It might be unwise to ignore him. Perhaps we should get on the right side of him now – take along a few gifts to prove our friendship… That sort of thing.
Balthazar	I've been thinking…
Caspar	Careful, now!
Balthazar	And I think this man must be more than just a king. The prophets have written about his birth. I'm going because I think we have a duty to do so.
Caspar	Oh dear, I really don't know what to do. If I'm away for a long time, then I think my brother may seize control while I'm absent. He's popular with the army, you see. Oh dear, oh dear. What a choice!
Balthazar	But don't you think we have a duty to go?
Caspar	What? Well, yes, I suppose so.
Melchior	I have the answer. I'll lend you my King's Bodyguard to take control in your absence. They'll stop your brother taking over.

Plays

Balthazar	And a few companies of my City Guards can help out as well. Now, does that make the choice easier?
Caspar	Well… yes, yes, it does. I'll come. A thousand thanks, my friends. Er… is the star still there? *(BALTHAZAR nods)* It is? Then we must leave, now. *(Starts to exit but BALTHAZAR restrains him)*
Balthazar	Steady. I hoped you would come and my servants are even now completing the preparations. We must take quite a lot with us. One thing, though. I beg you to travel with your minds on friendship – not fear, and not politics.
Melchior	Friendship, certainly, but politics as well, perhaps!
Balthazar	Astronomer, are they ready?
Astronomer	Yes, Sire. The servants have just finished. The camels are fully loaded and carry supplies for three months. We don't know where we will end up – only that we travel to the west.
Melchior	I presume, Balthazar, that we'll travel at night and rest up each day.
Balthazar	That's my plan, yes. When we enter another kingdom, we'll visit the king in case one of his wives has had the baby we're looking for.
Caspar	I still don't know about this. I've got things to do, letters to write…
Balthazar	Caspar, my old friend, you worry too much. We leave now, while the star is so clear. Waste not the moment!
Caspar	But… but…
Melchior	If we put all your buts together they'd stretch to the moon! A clear night, good food, good company and petrol in the camels. Let's move!
	Exit BALTHAZAR, MELCHIOR, CASPAR, ASTRONOMER and SERVANT
Fred	Adverts! Blasted adverts! That's all we need, just when it was getting interesting.
Bertha	Never mind, dear. You can go and do the washing up now.
Fred	Eh? Oh – yeah, well, I've just remembered I've got to go and…
Bertha	Wash up, you were going to say, weren't you. Come on – you wash and I'll wipe.
	Exeunt

Plays ✪

Scene Two

Enter FRED and BERTHA

Bertha   There. Now we can both relax with all the washing up done.

Fred   Bah! Ruined my hands, it has. We need a dishwasher. Now I've missed half of it!

Bertha   And if you're quiet you won't miss any more, will you! *(Sits and picks up knitting)*

Fred   Grrr! *(About to sit)* Got your knitting? Good. *(Sits)*

Sketch 3 – King Herod's palace

Enter HEROD, TWO GUARDS holding SLAVE, MINISTER 1 and MINISTER 2

Herod   What? What did you say?

Slave   Great King Herod! I cannot pay you back yet. I beg you for more time…

Herod   Dog! You dog! Take that! *(Pretends to hit SLAVE)* And that! *(Pretends to hit him again)* Hold him firmly, guards. Well, what do I do with him?

Minister 1   You cannot be lenient with him, Sire.

Herod   I haven't the slightest intention of being lenient. You are paid to give me useful advice, Minister. I suggest you earn your pay!

Minister 2   He must die, Your Majesty – as an example to others.

Herod   Of course he must die! The question is how!

Enter HEROD'S SERVANT, bowing low. HEROD'S SERVANT whispers in HEROD'S ear

Herod   Eh? Oh, I see. Send them in at once. At once! *(Exit HEROD'S SERVANT)* Throw him in the dungeons. I'll decide what to do with him later.

Slave   Spare me great king, spare me! My family will starve…

SLAVE is dragged off by the TWO GUARDS

Enter ASTRONOMER, followed by BALTHAZAR, CASPAR and MELCHIOR

Astronomer   Your gracious and most high Majesty, by your leave I will introduce my royal masters. King Balthazar…

Herod   Welcome to Jerusalem, King Balthazar.

❂ Plays

Balthazar	Thank you, King Herod.
Astronomer	King Caspar…
Herod	I am very happy to see you and your friends, King Caspar.
Caspar	Nice to be here, old chap!
Astronomer	And King Melchior.
Herod	You are welcome here, King Melchior.
Melchior	It is good of you to see us.
Herod	*(Calls off-stage)* Servants, wine for my guests! My friends – I hope I may call you that – I have heard of you and the lands you rule. I am honoured that you have called at my humble home.

HEROD'S SERVANT can re-enter and serve drinks during this scene if you wish

Balthazar	The honour is ours, Sire.
Caspar	We could not enter your kingdom without calling on you.
Herod	Good, good. Now, tell me the reason for your journey and visit.
Melchior	Well, strange as it seems, we've been following a star.
Caspar	It has led us here, to Jerusalem.
Melchior	Our astronomer forecast the birth of a great king…
Caspar	…and that his birth would be marked by a star.
Balthazar	*(Points out of window)* That is the star – you can see it from the window. Do you see? *(All move over to window)*
Herod	Ah, yes. The bright one.
Melchior	The star has led us this way.
Caspar	And since you are the king…
Melchior	And this is your palace…
Balthazar	Clearly, any prince would be born here, so we have come to pay our respects to your son, and then we'll be off home.
Herod	I have no new son, but I have also heard from my own people that a new king will be born.
Balthazar	But if the new king is not to be found here…
Caspar	In the royal palace…
Melchior	Then where can he be found?
Herod	I'd like to know the answer to that question, as well!
Balthazar	Friends, we must be quick! The star is moving again!

Plays ✪

40

Caspar	It's still going westward.
Melchior	We must get on our way again.
Balthazar	At once!
Caspar	Oh dear. I thought we'd be turning around soon.
Melchior	And so we shall, my friend. If we go much further this way, then we'll be in the sea!
Herod	*(Aside)* This is awkward. Not a happy situation at all! These fools have confirmed my fears. So some king has been born and will try to take over my kingdom, will he! *(Getting angry)* Over my dead body! Herod is king here and no other! *(Calming down)* But what will I do? I cannot imprison these kings – that would cause trouble and would not help me at all. Should I offer to travel with them? No… no… hmmm… Ah! I have it!
Balthazar	We must be on our way, King Herod.
Caspar	Many thanks for the hospitality, my dear fellow.
Melchior	We would like to stay, but the star calls us on, you see.
Herod	Of course, of course, my friends. If you would do me just one little favour, though, I'd be so very grateful.
Balthazar	It would be our pleasure.
Caspar	If we can help in any way…
Melchior	You only have to say the word.
Herod	You are too kind. I wish to visit this new and powerful king myself, but affairs of state do not allow me to leave my palace for long. When you've found him, how about stopping off here for a few days on your way home? We can get to know each other – we've only just met, after all. And you can tell me where the dear baby is and I can go and give him a prince's present. *(Twists his hands together, unseen by the other kings)*
Balthazar	An excellent idea.
Caspar	Capital plan.
Melchior	Couldn't be better. You could give us a guided tour of Jerusalem. It's an idea that might catch on.
Herod	*(Aside)* Fools! I've got them now! *(To kings)* Well, my friends, I won't delay you. Your camels are refuelled and you must be keen to get on.

Plays

Balthazar	True, we must get going.
Caspar	Toodlepip, old chap. See you soon.
Melchior	Time to hit the trail.
Herod	A safe journey to you.
	Exit MELCHIOR, CASPAR, BALTHAZAR and ASTRONOMER as HEROD waves
Herod	*(Laughs)* Well, my ministers. What did you think?
Minister 1	Oh, you were absolutely wonderful, Sire.
Minister 2	You had them eating out of your hand, Sire. It was wonderful to see.
Herod	What about my plan?
Minister 1	Your plan, Sire? Splendid. Really, brilliant. It's too complex for us to understand, of course, Sire.
Herod	Of course it is!
Minister 2	Those kings will tell you where this impostor is to be found…
Minister 1	We go and arrest him…
Minister 2	Put him and his parents in prison…
Minister 1	Where they'll never be heard of again!
Herod	Almost… almost… But you're wrong about the prison. *(Starts to shout)* I am king here! There will be no others – none! King Herod rules OK! All impostors must die!
Minister 1	Should we follow those kings?
Minister 2	To make sure they come back here and we know where they have been?
Herod	What? And frighten them off? I think not! We won't need to. They're looking forward to my offer of the best bed and breakfast in Jerusalem. Fools!
Minister 1	It's quite a brilliant plan, Sire. Now, what about the slave?
Herod	Slave? What slave?
Minister 2	The one you were dealing with when your visitors arrived.
Herod	Oh, him. Kill him, of course.
Minister 1	Yes, Majesty, but…
Minister 2	You always select the manner of death…
Herod	But I'm a happy man, now. Very happy. My problems and worries will soon be at an end. You can choose this time, but make sure he suffers, of course. As a warning to others.

Plays

© **pfp** publishing limited 2002 ISBN 1 874050 59 7 May be photocopied for use only within the purchasing institution **pfp**, 61 Gray's Inn Road, London WC1X 8TH

Ministers 1 & 2	Of course, Your Majesty.
	Exit HEROD, MINISTER 1 and MINISTER 2
Bertha	I'd love a cup of tea. *(Pause)* I said I'd love a cup of tea. Did you hear me?
Fred	Would you?
Bertha	Yes, I would.
Fred	Oh, yeah?
Bertha	Ever so much.
Fred	Oh, yes.
Bertha	Your turn for a change.
Fred	Oh, yeah?
Bertha	*(Annoyed)* So move yourself!
Fred	I don't know. There's no peace in this house… *(Exits and enters)* Where's the milk?
Bertha	Go on – you go and find it for yourself. I mean – where would you expect to find the milk?
Fred	In a cow? Honestly, what a life I lead… *(Sighs and exits)*
Bertha	*(Changes channel)* This looks better. I can't stand loud voices. Ooh look – there's that Mary again, and she's with other people round the campfire. I wonder if I can pick up the story… She shouldn't be roughing it like that, not with her being pregnant. Oh my – time has gone on – she looks ready to give birth. What does it say here? *(Picks up TV guide)* 'In those days a decree was issued by the Emperor Augustus for a general registration throughout the Roman world. For this purpose, everyone made his way to his own town, and so Joseph went up to Judaea, from the town of Nazareth, to be registered at the City of David, called Bethlehem, because he was of the House of David by descent. And with him went Mary…'
	Enter MARY, JOSEPH and TRAVELLERS. They start to get in position for the start of the next sketch, sitting round a campfire
Bertha	I wonder which of those men is Joseph. Perhaps he's that nice-looking one there… *(Points to one of the TRAVELLERS)*
Joseph	*(Who has not yet sat down)* Actually, I'm Joseph, OK? I don't really know who these people are. The whole country seems to

Plays

be on the move and we've just linked up with them for the night. I always say 'there's safety in numbers', and with Mary in her condition… well… you can never be too careful. So – can we get on? We're quite anxious to start this bit. Are you sitting comfortably, Mrs Higginbottom? *(Sits with MARY and TRAVELLERS)*

Bertha Lovely, thank you, young man. *(Aside)* Coo… I've never had anyone on telly talking to me before, have you?

Sketch 4 – A campfire by the road to Bethlehem

Traveller 1 Well, I say a curse on Caesar for his census!

Traveller 2 It's completely disrupted our way of life, that's for sure.

Traveller 3 My business may be ruined by the time I get home. I'm a fruit grower and I've got work to do.

Traveller 1 And what about the rest of us? I cure leather and I've got hides soaking in vats. They'll rot if I'm not there to take them out. *(To TRAVELLER 2)* What about you?

Traveller 2 Well, let's just say my business involves making money, and as long as I'm on this little holiday courtesy of Caesar Augustus I'm not making a dinaro.

Joseph Well, I suppose the Romans know what they're doing. We have to obey the law even if we don't agree with it.

Traveller 3 Whose side are you on, mate?

Traveller 1 Let's put it this way. The Romans are foreigners, right? I mean, they invaded our country. That makes them enemies. I don't like to be bossed around by enemies, right?

Joseph Oh, yes. I see your point of view.

Traveller 2 And I don't like the threats they've made if we don't comply.

Traveller 3 Yes – transportation, slavery or death. Some choice!

Joseph Certainly, it's not the most considerate of laws – not at the moment, anyway.

Traveller 1 *(To MARY)* It must be a real pain for you – if you'll forgive me for saying so, lady.

Traveller 2 A lady in your condition shouldn't be out here in the wilds for any reason.

Plays ✪

44

Traveller 3	Only yesterday, three travellers were killed by robbers in the last village.
Traveller 1	That's why we've made a point of travelling together.
Traveller 2	But there are only two of you. Doesn't that alarm you?
Joseph	Yes.
	(Said together)
Mary	No.
Joseph	*(Sharply)* Of course I'm blasted well worried… sorry – I shouldn't have bitten your head off. I'm worried sick, but as you heard, my wife thinks she's got a special sort of protection.
Traveller 1	Is this right, lady?
Mary	Yes, I'm sure of it.
Traveller 2	But how? Your husband may be fit and strong but…
Traveller 3	He can't protect you from murderers.
Mary	God will protect me.
Traveller 1	Well, yes. I admire your faith, but we all pray for God's protection.
Traveller 3	I'm afraid God's protection didn't work for those poor devils who were robbed and murdered yesterday.
Mary	I can't explain how I know that God will protect me – I just do.
Joseph	Don't try to argue with her. She has a deep belief which amazes me.
Traveller 2	It's refreshing to find such a strong faith these days.
Traveller 3	Tell me – where are you from?
Joseph	Nazareth. Do you know it?
Traveller 1	Nazareth? I've never been there, but you've certainly had a journey and a half!
Traveller 3	And where are you heading tomorrow?
Joseph	Well, that's the one good thing about it. We hope to reach Bethlehem tomorrow. I don't think my wife could stand more than that on these tracks.
Traveller 1	Oh well, you're almost there, then. *(Points)* It's just beyond that hill over there – a day's walk.
Traveller 2	That's where I've just come from.

❂ **Plays**

Traveller 3	There's one big problem you'll have to face, though. The whole place is crawling with people who've had to report there. You don't stand a chance of finding a hotel room – or anywhere else to stay.
Joseph	Thanks for the comforting thought!
Traveller 1	Have you got relations there who can put you up?
Joseph	No, I'm afraid we haven't. Never mind. We'll find somewhere…
Traveller 2	Well, I wish you luck. Maybe the lady will bring you some.
Mary	I'm sure we'll find somewhere. Joseph, don't you think we should sleep now?
Joseph	Yes, you're quite right, Mary. Are you comfortable as you are?
Mary	Yes, thanks. I'm as snug as a bug in a rug, but what about you?
Joseph	I'm fine, dear – now go to sleep. You look exhausted. *(Turns to TRAVELLERS)* Do you think we ought to keep watch?
Traveller 2	Yes, and keep the fire going to scare off the wild animals.
Traveller 3	Someone was eaten by a lion near here last week.
Traveller 1	What a little ray of sunshine you are – what with robbers and man-eating animals! Anytime I feel like being cheered up, I'll come and find you!
Joseph	I'll take the first watch, if you like.
Traveller 1	I'll take over from you if you wake me.
Traveller 2	OK, I'll do the next stint.
Traveller 3	Then I'll keep watch until dawn. Right – best get to counting sheep – that's how I get to sleep. Sleep well, my friends.
Traveller 1	Wake me in a couple of hours. Goodnight.
Joseph	Goodnight.

Exit TRAVELLERS, MARY and JOSEPH

Enter FRED with two cups. He hands one to BERTHA

Fred	Here you are, love. Nice cup of tea, made with my own little hands. *(Sits)*

Plays ✪

© **pfp** publishing limited 2002 ISBN 1 874050 59 7 May be photocopied for use only within the purchasing institution **pfp**, 61 Gray's Inn Road, London WC1X 8TH

46

☆What's on tonight, dear?

Bertha	Thank you, Fred – that was kind of you.

Enter SON

Bertha	Hello, son. Had a nice evening, dear?
Son	Yeah, Mum.
Fred	Been out with your girlfriend, son?
Son	Yeah, Dad.
Fred	Which one, son?
Son	Lily, Dad.
Fred	Lily? Cor – she's a bit of alright!
Bertha	Want to watch the telly, dear?
Son	Yeah, Mum. *(Sits on floor in front of chairs)*
Fred	Not very exciting, son. Crowd of twits running around in their nightshirts…
Bertha and son	Shhhhhhhhhhhhhhhhhhhhhhhhhhh!!

Sketch 5 – Bethlehem town centre

Enter BETHLEHEM CROWD, MARY and JOSEPH. INNKEEPERS to be behind 'doors'

Mary	They didn't exaggerate, did they? Look at them all!
Joseph	People from all over the place! Curse the Roman Emperor.
Mary	No, Joseph. Don't say that. I'm sure he had a very good reason.
Joseph	You stay here, Mary. I'll go and see what can be done. You sit in the shade here a moment. I won't be long.

MARY goes to stage side. JOSEPH wanders, looking for inns and knocks on first door

Innkeeper 1	Yeah? What do you want, then?
Joseph	Sorry to bother you. I expect you're very busy, but I wonder if you have a room for the night? We're here for the census and my wife's pregnant…
Innkeeper 1	So? That's tough. You some kind of funny guy? Look at the place – crawling with people and you ask if I've got room?
Joseph	I'm sorry. I only asked if…
Innkeeper 1	Yeah, well, don't. There's no room anywhere. Push off.

☆ Plays

JOSEPH continues and knocks at the second door

Innkeeper 2	If you want a room, stranger, the answer's no. I'm sorry, but I can't help you. I'm absolutely packed out. I've already doubled the number in each room. The district council would have a fit if they knew!
Joseph	Oh dear. My wife is going to have a baby any time now and we're getting desperate. We must find somewhere!
Innkeeper 2	I'd really like to help you but we're bulging at the seams. We've even got guests in our part of the inn. I tell you – the only place we've got where someone could lie down tonight is the stable with the animals.
Joseph	Oh – I see. Well, thank you, anyway. *(Aside)* Now what on earth do I do?
Bertha	Oh, the poor man.
Fred	Eh?
Bertha	Well, he's all worried.
Fred	Oh.
Bertha	I mean, it's not right.
Fred	Eh?
Bertha	I mean, the council should have helped.
Fred	Oh.
Son	Shhhhhhhhhhhhhhhhhhhhh!!
Joseph	It's no use, Mary. I've tried all the inns and they're full. I can't even find a bed and breakfast with any rooms free.
Mary	I'm sorry to cause you so much worry, Joseph, but we must have somewhere, and quickly. It won't be very long now. *(Holds tummy)* When a baby's got to come, a baby's got to come!
Joseph	But there's nothing. Our son is going to be born in the corner of a field. One joker suggested we could use his stable. Honestly, what a…
Mary	We'll take it.
Joseph	What? But you can't make do with a stable!
Mary	Much better than the corner of a field, Joseph. Come on – take me there – quickly, before someone else grabs it… Hurry!

MARY and JOSEPH move through crowd towards INNKEEPER 2, but not in a straight line

Plays ✪

48

Innkeeper 2	Hello, again. I'm afraid that nobody has lef…
Joseph	We'll take it – the stable, I mean. It'll be fine – wonderful!
Innkeeper 2	The stable? But…
Joseph	Yes, we'll take it.
Innkeeper 2	The stable?
Mary	*(With forced patience)* Yes, the stable.
Innkeeper 2	But I was only joking. I mean… you can't have a baby in a stable… What will the neighbours say if they find out? I mean…
Mary	Please? We must have somewhere.
Joseph	We'll pay, of course.
Innkeeper 2	Bless you, sir! I wouldn't charge for a stable. Well… I could put some fresh straw down, I suppose, and shift the donkey over a bit. I've got some clean blankets.
Joseph	We've spent the last few nights outside. This will seem luxurious, I can tell you, and some clean water would make it a home from home.
Innkeeper 2	Right, then. Sir, madam, if you'll come this way, please. Mind your head on the beam, there. This way…

Exit BETHLEHEM CROWD, INNKEEPERS, MARY and JOSEPH

Fred	Oh no! Just look at that. Picture's gone!
Son	Clever, Dad. We can see it's gone.
Bertha	Well, do something about it. Quickly, then or we'll lose the story.
Fred	Keep your hair on. *(Gets up and goes to TV)* Let's try the subtle approach. *(Bangs TV)* No. That didn't work.
Son	What about the horizontal hold, Dad? Try that.
Fred	Yeah, OK. Don't suppose anyone would like to make me another cup of tea while I'm trying to fix this for you? Oh… er… *(To audience)* Normal service will be resumed as soon as possible.

Exeunt

INTERVAL

Plays

Scene Three

Enter FRED, BERTHA and SON. FRED and SON are standing over the TV

Son	I told you, Dad.
Fred	I was about to twiddle that knob.
Son	Yeah, likely!
Fred	I was! It was the next thing to try. You young people rush things. You've got to do these things systematically…
Bertha	Well, why don't you two sit down systematically and then we can see what's on. *(They go back to the chairs and sit as before)*
Son	It's changed channels…
Fred	That's because I can't get a picture on the one we were watching.
Bertha	I think it'll be about a load of shepherds.
Son	Eh? Why?
Bertha	There are always shepherds at Christmas. I don't know where they are for the rest of the year, but they wheel them out at Christmas.
Son	*(Looks at TV guide)* You're right! Cor, my mum's clever!
Fred	Here they are – all sitting around a fire. As usual, though, there's not much happening. *(Yawns)*

Sketch 6 – A hillside near Bethlehem

Enter SHEPHERDS. All are sitting round a fire, except for SHEPHERD 5 who is over to side of stage

Shepherd 1	Well, are you satisfied now?
Shepherd 2	No, I'm not. I'm convinced there's something out there. The flock are all restless tonight.
Shepherd 1	Oh, stop moaning – they're OK.
Shepherd 2	Listen, you. Who's in charge here? Me! Who carries the can if we lose any sheep, eh? Me! So don't tell me I'm moaning!
Shepherd 3	Ah, don't worry about him – he's got girlfriend trouble – he can't help it.
Shepherd 2	If I've got girlfriend trouble that's my affair – got it? Not yours, or yours. Keep your noses out of it.

Plays ✪

☆What's on tonight, dear?

Shepherd 1	Hey – settle down you two. Let's have a bit of peace and harmony.
Shepherd 4	Chill out, man. Get the cools.
Shepherd 2	Yeah, well. Sorry.
Shepherd 3	OK, OK.
	Pause
Shepherd 4	Nice weather for the time of year…
Shepherd 2	Have you tried crossing the street in Bethlehem these days?
Shepherd 3	You stand a good chance of being crushed to death!
Shepherd 4	My uncle stands to make a lot of money out of this census. I heard him say that a couple more weeks like this and he could retire.
Shepherd 1	What's he charging the guests per night?
Shepherd 4	That is private business. MYOB.
Shepherd 2	Well, I say good old Emperor. After all – it's great for business. All the shops and pubs are flourishing – they've never had so many customers.
Shepherd 1	Look out – here comes Seth.
	SHEPHERD 5 comes towards main group
Shepherd 5	Typical. Absolutely typical. I'm cold, fed up with staring at sheep and the bloke who should have taken over from me is roasting his tootsies, snug by the fire. Typical.
Shepherd 1	Sorry, Seth – my fault. I got a bit comfortable sitting by the fire and since wristwatches haven't been invented yet I lost track of time. I'm on my way.
Shepherd 5	Nothing happened, but the sheep seem a bit uneasy tonight.
Shepherd 2	Told you! There's something wrong. I know it.
Shepherd 1	OK. I'll keep my eyes peeled just for you, Boss!
	SHEPHERD 1 moves to side
Shepherd 3	Toss another log on the fire, someone. *(SHEPHERD 5 does so as he sits down)*
Shepherd 1	*(At side of stage)* Cor, it's cold away from the fire. I'll keep moving… I can see why Seth was cheesed off with me… *(Wanders at side of stage)* They seem to all be here. Hello, sheep,

Plays

	how are you? Are you having a nice evening? Well, answer me, then. What's your name? Are you called sheep? And you? Wow! This is exciting!… Nice evening… Lovely sky. *(Looks around at sky)* Oh, my! That star is so bright! It's… it's moving, I think. Yes… it's moving. It's growing… getting nearer and bigger… I must tell the others. I bet the dozy lot haven't seen it. *(Runs to others)*
Shepherd 4	Hey! What about the sheep?
Shepherd 2	Wolves? Is it wolves?
Shepherd 1	No – not wolves. It's that star up there. It's coming towards us – look!
Shepherd 3	Wow – it's so bright! But it's not a star. I don't think it can be. There's a shape in it, do you see?
Shepherd 4	I can see a man. Oh heck! What does it mean?

Enter ANGEL, slowly

Shepherd 3	No good for a start. This is an evil sign – a bad omen.
Shepherd 4	We're doomed!
Shepherd 1	It's stopped… and it's turning towards us… this means big trouble!
Shepherd 3	We must do something to protect ourselves.
Shepherd 4	Quick – on your knees.

SHEPHERDS kneel and cower, looking at the ground

Shepherd 2	May we be spared!
Angel	Shepherds – do not be scared. No harm will come to you.
Shepherd 4	*(Aside)* Don't be scared, he says!
Angel	Do I look as though I'm going to bash you on the head? Look at me. *(SHEPHERDS look at ANGEL)* That's better. I have splendid news for you. A great Messiah has been given to the people…
Shepherds	A Messiah?
Angel	Yes. This Messiah, this leader from God, can be found as a newborn baby in a stable in Bethlehem. Go and visit him. You see – there is no need to be scared. Glory to God in the highest And on earth, peace To all those who have found his favour.

Plays ✪

(Aside) There. I've said my lines, and they don't look scared anymore. You've got to put yourself in these shepherds' shoes… well, they probably wore sandals, actually, but what I mean is, they didn't live in a world of electric lights. People were dead scared of the night, you know. Ghouls and ghosts and goodness knows what used to roam the dark in their imaginations! I seem to frighten everyone I meet. I hope I haven't frightened you. I've got lots of lovely messages to dish out – that's all. Cheerio! Oh – sorry about the lack of radiant light – we couldn't quite manage that. 'Bye!

Exit ANGEL. The SHEPHERDS start to stand up

Shepherd 1	It's fading.
Shepherd 2	Imagination. Sheer imagination.
Shepherd 3	But I've barely touched the wine!
Shepherd 4	No imagination. We all saw it. That was real.
Shepherd 5	Go to Bethlehem, we were told. We must obey. That must have been a messenger from God.
Shepherd 1	I'll go.
Shepherd 3	And me.
Shepherds 4 & 5	And we'll come.
Shepherd 2	Hold it, hold it. I'll decide who goes. Right, then – *(To SHEPHERDS 1 and 3)* you two stay – you're on duty. I'll go and *(To SHEPHERDS 4 and 5)* you two can come with me.
Shepherd 3	You must take a gift.
Shepherd 2	What? Shepherds like us? We can't afford precious jewels. If he comes from God he'll want rich treasures…
Shepherd 3	But we're not ashamed of being shepherds.
Shepherd 2	True. Well said. *(Thinks)* We'll take a lamb.
Shepherd 4	That is worth a great deal to us.
Shepherd 1	And we have to stay here.
Shepherd 3	As blooming usual.
Shepherd 1	While you get all the fun.
Shepherd 3	And we freeze and do all the work.
Shepherds 1 & 3	As blooming usual.
Shepherd 2	Any more of that and I'll have you on extra night duties, got it? Right, let's go. We'll pick up a lamb on our way.

Plays ✪

All you need for Christmas

Exit SHEPHERDS.

Fred	Alright if I turn over, now, love? I want to see the end of the news.
Bertha	OK with me, Fred. What about you, dear?
Son	Yeah, Mum.
Fred	Like to see the news, don't you, son?
Son	Yeah, Dad.
Fred	Switch it over, then, son.
Son	Why should I, Dad?
Fred	Don't you talk to me like that, son!
Son	Sorry, Dad.
Bertha	Do it yourself, Fred. Don't you bully my poor little boy!
Fred	*(Getting up to change the TV channel. Muttering)* Cor, I don't know. Keep a dog and bark yourself! Come to think of it – it was the dog that chewed up the remote…

Sketch 7 – The Nativity, a stable in Bethlehem

Enter MARY and JOSEPH with baby Jesus (centre stage), REPORTER (at front to one side), with room for cast of Nativity scene behind – SHEPHERDS 2, 4 and 5, BALTHAZAR, CASPAR, MELCHIOR. The animals could be played by other cast members.

Reporter	And we join News at Ten just as things are beginning to happen here, in downtown Bethlehem. As the cameras cover this bare, simple stable, I wonder if you, the viewers, can imagine the atmosphere in this place There, in the centre, you can see Mary and Joseph and, of course, the reason why the world's media is here tonight – the baby Jesus. Yes, we can confirm that the proud parents have decided to name him 'Jesus'. We understand that this name was selected many months ago. Behind and to the left are the animals that normally occupy this part of the stable. They were, only a short time ago, silent witnesses to the greatest miracle since the creation of the world. They witnessed the birth of God's son, a birth not in a palace but in a humble stable, with cobwebs, animal smells and straw. God has come among the ordinary people with this

Plays ✪

54

birth to give them his message for the world… and… hold on… *(Listening in)* wow… that was quick.

Enter SHEPHERDS 2, 4 and 5

Here they are, now. Shepherds from the hills around Bethlehem. Looking hot and weary, they hesitantly come forward and – look – they are leaving a gift – a lamb. *(SHEPHERDS 2, 4 and 5 present their gift to Jesus)*
And I have just heard a group of VIP visitors has arrived and is being escorted into the stable by a very proud innkeeper… yes, here they are now.

Enter BALTHAZAR, CASPAR, MELCHIOR and INNKEEPER 2

You may recognise King Balthazar, King Caspar and King Melchior as they step forward and present gifts to the new-born baby, gifts which he will not understand for many a year. Gold… frankincense… and myrrh. Yes, there they go – one after the other… *(They present their gifts to Jesus)*
I wish you could capture the atmosphere – so hushed – and yet so full of joy. I wonder what thoughts are in King Melchior's head. Remember, he came to make an alliance with a new king and, instead, finds himself in a stable, with a group of shepherds, presenting his gift to a baby! Ideas of political alliances have gone out the window now, I should think…
Look at the contrast between these two groups of visitors. This tiny baby has received homage from the rich and the poor, from rulers and the ruled. Clearly, Jesus will have an interesting life ahead of him. This is *(name of REPORTER)* returning you to the studio.

Exit BALTHAZAR, CASPAR, MELCHIOR, INNKEEPER, SHEPHERDS, JOSEPH, MARY and REPORTER

Fred	It's only the weather forecast now and that's always wrong. I'm off to bed. *(Gets up)*
Bertha	Yes, me too. We've had a very busy evening. *(Gets up)*
Fred	You coming, son?
Son	No, Dad.

❁ **Plays**

Bertha	Want to watch more telly, dear?
Son	Yeah, Mum.
Fred	Switch it off when you're finished, then, son.
Son	OK, Dad.
Bertha	Night, then, dear.
Son	Night, Mum. Night, Dad.

Exit FRED and BERTHA

Enter REPORTER

Reporter Here is a newsflash. It has been disclosed within the last few minutes that troops operating under the direct orders of King Herod are killing all male babies without exception in a wide area around Jerusalem. It is believed that this action is being taken because of a possible plot against the royal family. A spokesman at the palace expressed regret that this action has been necessary and continued to say that the king felt sure he would continue to enjoy the love and affection of his subjects.

Reports are coming in of at least one group of refugees who were able to slip through the army cordon placed around the region. It is thought that Joseph the carpenter, of Nazareth, and his family are among the escapees, but we are unable to confirm these details. We will, of course, keep you informed throughout the evening of any further developments in this story. This is the end of the newsflash.

Exit REPORTER

SON switches off TV. Prepares for bed. Enter FRED

Fred You know, son, I've been thinking. That story… all those kings and shepherds and so on… It was a bit, sort of, like that Christmas story, don't you think?

Son Oh, Dad – how do you do it, eh? *(Puts arm on FRED's shoulder and gently guides him off-stage to bed.)*

Exeunt.

CURTAIN

Plays ✪

pfp

The twitching curtain

This assembly seeks to deal with the issue of loneliness at Christmas.

Resources

A display of happy Christmas pictures, photographs and cards would be an advantage in setting the scene but are not essential.

Introduction

If I said the word 'Christmas', I bet all sorts of lovely ideas would leap into your mind. I bet there would be lots of you putting your hands in the air to share your thoughts, as well. Let's find out, shall we?

Christmas! Now then – what does that word make you think of?
(*Take a range of responses from the children, giving particular recognition to any that display a sense of appreciation or caring.*)

OK – thank you. Just think back to all those responses and the different things they covered. I can see that you are really looking forward to Christmas. Hands up who'd like it to be Christmas tomorrow. There you are then. What did I tell you!

I'm going to read a short story now. I want you to think about how your sort of Christmas compares to the one Mrs Saro is expecting.

Story

John and Josie – and their parents, dog and two cats – moved into their new home in late November. It was bigger than their last place and there was room to move around.

Best of all was the garden where they could 'let off steam', as their dad put it.

The family hadn't moved far (just round the corner, really) and so they still went to the same school and had the same friends, which was really great. In fact, the first Saturday after the move several friends came round to check out the new house and have a bit of a kick around in the garden. As they were leaving, one of Josie's friends, Sarita, spoke to her quietly.

'How do you put up with it?' she asked. 'I mean, being watched all the time?'

Josie looked shocked. 'What do you mean – watched?' she asked.

'The curtains next door keep moving. I'm sure there's someone standing there watching us. See what I mean?'

Josie darted a quick glance at the neighbour's house in time to see the bottom corner of the net curtain fall back into place. 'I see what you mean,' she said nervously, worried that she hadn't noticed a thing before.

After that, every time she left the back door she checked the windows for signs of life and often saw the give-away twitch of the net. She found it spooky and at supper she asked her mum who lived next door.

'Oh, I think an old lady lives there,' replied Mum as she sat down. 'Why do you ask?' Josie told everyone about what Sarita had seen and how she'd seen the curtains moving too.

'I think there's a ghost in the house,' declared John and rose with his arms reaching forward, pulling a scary face.

'Sit down – you'll put us off our supper!' said Dad as he gently pushed him down. 'She's not a ghost. I've met her. She's just a friendly old lady who lives alone.'

'That's right,' added Mum. 'She probably *was* watching you. She doesn't have much else to do. Anyway, you'll meet her soon enough. Now then John, eat some more cabbage. It'll put hairs on your chest!'

In fact the children didn't have long to wait before meeting their neighbour. The next day Josie kicked the ball too hard and – yes – it zoomed over the fence and straight into the middle of the next door garden. After arguing about who should go round to ask for the ball back they decided that they would both go.

Josie in particular felt very nervous as they heard a distant shuffling and a rattle as the door handle moved and the door slowly opened. But then the feeling left her, because the old lady who stood in the doorway looked just like their granny. She wore a thick jumper, tweed skirt and on her feet had bright tiger-design slippers.

'Hello. You must be Josie, and you're John,' she said. 'I've heard all about you from your dad.' Josie groaned inwardly – she could just imagine what he'd have said! 'I'm Mrs Saro and I bet I know why you're here,' the old lady continued.

Of course there was no problem about retrieving the ball. In fact she told them to come around and fetch it whenever they needed to. The children thanked Mrs Saro, collected the ball and returned to their own house. Occasionally the ball went over and they went to fetch it. Gradually, they started to wave when they saw the net curtain move, and it wasn't long before the curtain was actually pulled aside to reveal Mrs Saro waving back. She really enjoyed having children next door!

As Christmas came nearer, decorations appeared and groups of carol singers were in the streets. School had ended with a big party and Josie and John couldn't wait for Christmas Day. Time seemed to go slower the closer it got to Christmas! The last presents had been bought and John was trying to finish writing his Christmas cards.

'Did you send one to Mrs Saro?' he asked.

'Yes,' replied Josie. She was quiet for a bit. 'I wonder what she's doing about Christmas?'

'Going to her family, I expect,' said John as he chewed the end of his pen.

But Josie knew she wasn't because she'd heard Dad say she hadn't any family left. She felt uncomfortable and uneasy about this. If she had no family… and no one ever seemed to call… then what sort of Christmas would Mrs Saro have?

Josie was lost in her thoughts for a while before she bounded out to the kitchen, where she found Mum. John could hear very little of their conversation, but he did hear Mum say, 'We thought the same, Josie. Go on – you ask. She'd love it, coming from you.'

Josie grabbed John with a quick 'C'mon!' and they raced next door.

Mrs Saro opened the door and invited them in, now that she knew the parents would not mind. She listened in complete silence as Josie asked her question. Her jaw seemed to tighten and her eyelids filled. Perhaps she'd been offended – but then a small, shaky smile appeared and a quavery voice whispered, 'Thank you.'

Christmas Day was as good as everyone had expected. The house had been a scene of frantic activity all morning, but now the meal was under way and they were pulling crackers. John had put crumbs out for the birds and – if a cheeky robin had chosen to look through the window – it would have seen five humans wearing paper hats and laughing their heads off. Mum, Dad, John and Josie and – there, in the middle of the family – Mrs Saro.

From a scary beginning, the children came to know their neighbour and to want to help her. They learned that she was lonely and realised they could make her happy by asking her to join them on Christmas Day.

Assemblies ✪

☆The twitching curtain

Conclusion

It's really important to help other people, but remember that you should only approach adults with your parents' permission. In this story, Josie and John told their parents what they were doing.

Prayer

Lord, in all our excitement and enjoyment, surrounded by our family members, help us to remember the lonely and the sad. It's very easy to forget that some can be on their own, even when surrounded by people. May we do something to bring the happiness of Christmas to lonely people. Amen.

Thought

Christmas is about giving – giving our time, our help, our friendship and, of course, presents to the people we love and care about. It's also a time when we receive presents and have a great time. Let's try our best to make it a great time for everyone by helping and caring for those around us.

Carol

'Good King Wenceslas'

Assemblies

Hilary's decision

This assembly centres on the choice a girl has to make between her own wishes and the needs of others at Christmas time.

Resources

School Christmas tree – placed near to the speaker.

Introduction

Well now, are you good at sharing your things? What about your favourite toys?
(Take responses.)

Now think of this. Pretend you've got something that is very precious to you. You want to keep it for ever, but other people need it and it could make them really happy. Would you share it?
(Take further responses.)

Listen to this story and then ask yourself if you would have made the same decision as Hilary in the story.

Story

Hilary loved her tree. Absolutely adored it. Now, I know that most people love their parents, their relations, their pets, their bikes, Playstations and maybe even their brothers or sisters! Hilary loved that lot as well, but she also loved her tree.

You see, it really was *her* tree. She had been born on Christmas Eve ten years before, and although she couldn't remember that Christmas, her parents had planted the Christmas tree in the garden after the decorations had been taken down. At first it had been quite small, but from Hilary's first wobbly steps into the garden she had been told it was her tree. She had watched it grow… and grow… and grow! Now it towered over the other plants in the garden and was over three metres tall.

Underneath its sweeping branches, Hilary had made a den which remained dry in all but the heaviest showers. She could see it from her bedroom and loved to watch it in all weathers. Her favourite time of year was in late spring when lime-green buds appeared at the tips of the branches, and she knew the tree was about to start growing again.

Hilary's older brother, Simon, had suggested a few years ago that she should dig up the 'stupid tree' and put it in a pot for Christmas, but Hilary was so upset by the thought that in the end the idea had gone away. From then on, she had put decorations on the tree each Christmas.

All Hilary's friends thought she was a bit potty to feel like this about a tree – 'two slices short of a loaf' as they used to say. But it made no difference and it didn't stop her being popular. In fact, her friends liked the idea of having a weird friend!

Hilary's other love was being a member of the church choir in St Hugh's. She was a junior member and occupied the front choirstalls with some other children, while a row of grown ups filled the row behind and made sure they didn't natter during the sermon!

Hilary was in her place in plenty of time for the choir practice on the 23rd of

☆Hilary's decison

December because it was the last run-through of all the Christmas music.

Mrs Snelling, the choir mistress, tapped her baton on the music stand to indicate that the practice was about to begin and the noise died away, leaving old Mr Lymes laughing on his own at a joke someone had made in the back row.

The practice got under way and Hilary became so involved in the music and the need to get the anthem right that it was some time before she noticed a small group had gathered at the back of the church, centred on the rector, the Reverend Perry. There was a lot of frowning and scratching of heads going on and the rector was looking quite concerned.

'Hilary! Pay attention!' Mrs Snelling's voice jerked her back to the singing and Hilary buried her face in her music to cover the embarrassment now blooming on her face.

It turned out to be the last piece of music to be rehearsed that evening and Mrs Snelling ran over the arrangements for Christmas Eve and Christmas Day. Just as she was dismissing the choir Revd Perry appeared at her side.

'Mrs Snelling, I wonder if I could just have a quick word with everybody before they go…? Thank you.' He looked worried and searched for his words carefully before speaking. 'Um… I'm afraid that a bit of a problem has occurred. It's very sad, but there it is… You know that Mr Onions normally provides the church with a Christmas tree each year… well, I'm afraid that he's been taken to hospital because he is very ill…' Mr Perry waited for the buzz of conversation to die away, '…and we can't just chop down one of his trees without asking Mr Onions. We can't do that at the moment, so… I'm afraid we won't be having a tree this year…' His voice trailed away briefly. 'Er… I know that all you

children were planning to decorate it tomorrow afternoon…'

'Let's buy one!' called out Miss Hemmings. 'They've got very nice ones in the Co-op.'

'Yes, but in the church we need a tall tree,' said Mr Lymes. 'Theirs aren't over a metre tall.'

'No – I agree. We need a large one,' added Reverend Perry. 'But the simple truth is that we don't have enough money to buy a large tree and we can't just go and chop one down without its owners' permission. Oh well, it's not to be – but it's so lovely to see all the presents for the orphanage piled up at the bottom of a tree – and it's such a joy for singing carols around. Thank you all.'

Everyone prepared to go home, but Hilary was rooted to the spot, a frown on her forehead. From the moment the rector had made his announcement she had known what she ought to do. She had become like two different people. One Hilary felt that this was an opportunity to give other people happiness and therefore do some good. The other person within her was resentful – even angry – that as a result of Mr Onions being carted off to hospital she might have to lose her favourite and much-loved tree.

Thoughts see-sawed across her mind and she rose, determined not to weaken and hand over her tree. Eyes down in case anyone would look at her and think of the tree in her garden, Hilary made her way down the church towards the porch.

'I don't have to!' she told herself. 'So what if the church hasn't got a tree? They're not having mine!' and she stepped smartly through the porch.

'Goodnight, Hilary. Thanks for turning up,' said Reverend Perry, who was bringing a box in from his car. 'I'm really sorry there won't be a tree…'

'Er… Reverend Perry?'

★ Assemblies

'Yes, Hilary?'

'Er… *(No! Don't say it! Stop it! wheedled the other Hilary in her head)* Er… I've… got a Christmas tree.'

'A tree? Oh yes, the one in your garden? Yes, it's lovely, but that's your special tree. We all know about that tree, Hilary. We can't ask you for that one.'

'No, I *want* the church to have it.' Hilary paused, fighting the other voice inside her. 'I know it's getting too big for the garden now, if I'm honest, and I know that everyone else thinks so. It wouldn't seem like Christmas if we didn't have a tree in the church. I want the church to have it.'

Reverend Perry stood still and gazed at Hilary. 'Thank you, my dear,' he said. 'A tree does make Christmas, doesn't it. I think we'd better talk to your parents first though – just in case!'

Hilary's parents raised no objection because it was Hilary's tree. Hilary didn't look while it was chopped down – she couldn't. But when it arrived in church and she saw all the joy and happiness on everyone's faces she was glad of the decision she had made.

And do you know what? Underneath the old tree, very weak and barely alive due to lack of light, Hilary found a small seedling. Her tree would live on!

Conclusion

Sometimes we know exactly what we must do to help others but we avoid doing it because it goes against our selfish wishes. Hilary fought against the selfishness within her and gave her tree to the church so that many would share in enjoying it. She knew that it was better for all those people to enjoy her tree than to keep it to herself. And it made her happy too.

We need to listen to the voice inside us which tells us the right thing to do!

Prayer

Lord Jesus, you shared all you had with us. At this time we all share in the wonderful celebration of your birth. Help us to be sharers in life. May we do good for others this Christmas so that we may become more like you. Amen.

Thought

Sharers are carers. It takes a strong person to share what they have with other people. Let's make the decision to share our happiness with other people this Christmas. Wherever we go, let's try to make people happy!

Carol

'Deck the Halls with Boughs of Holly'

Assemblies ✪

Herbert the Christmas mouse

An assembly story for younger children that aims to bring to life the celebration of Christ's birth.

Resources

Nativity scene.

Introduction

I bet you can tell me the names of lots of the people in the Christmas story. Can you? *(Take responses.)*

That's terrific. Well done. But you know – I'm a bit disappointed. None of you have mentioned Herbert. Don't you know Herbert?

(Take responses. Have a bit of fun with this one!)

Well, you do surprise me! I mean – everyone's heard of Herbert – it says so here! Herbert was a mouse – yes, a mouse! One night he took shelter in a stable in a small town in another country... Well, here's the whole story.

Story

If you've ever lived on a farm or been allowed to explore one, you'll know that there are millions of places where something as small as a mouse can hide for ages. One of the best places is in a barn where the bales are heaped high and there are places that are never disturbed.

Well, the same sort of places could be found in old-fashioned stables – if you were very small and very quiet – just like Herbert.

Let me introduce him to you. Herbert was an ordinary mousy-looking mouse who liked mousy places to sniff about in and mousy food to nibble.

Herbert had never meant to live in a town – even a small town. If he hadn't been so nosy he could have been racing around among the rocks out in the countryside where he belonged. But oh no – he'd had to stick his long nose into things (into someone's sack, to be exact) and before he could say 'Wash my whiskers!' he'd been trapped as the owner had picked it up and tied it to his back. Then it was bump after bump until at last the sack had been put down and he'd managed to escape. Some escape! He was in a sort of town and there were so many of those great big 'people' things walking around that he only just made it to a wall without being trampled to death!

Scurrying along the bottom of the wall, Herbert had turned into the first doorway he found – only to come face to face with the meanest, scruffiest cat he'd ever seen. Cat? More like a sabre-toothed tiger, Herbert thought – not that he'd ever seen one! Herbert, of course, ran away quickly or he'd have had no tail – and no tale to tell. Dodging huge feet he zoomed up the street and under an old wooden door to find himself in a stable yard. Swiftly, he looked around. Perfect! Lots of cover for him to hide in. Dashing across the yard he buried himself in old, dry hay and waited for his heartbeat to slow down a bit. Then he began to search his new home – slowly and carefully. He quickly found food in various corners. Nice! Yes, he was going to be very comfortable here! Eating until he could swallow no more he found a dark corner to curl up in and went to sleep.

❂ **Assemblies**

Assemblies ✪

'Oi! Oi you! Get up!' Dimly, Herbert began to realise that this yelling was aimed at him and he stood up to find an unfriendly-looking mouse towering over him.

'Can I help you?' asked Herbert, rubbing the sleep from his eyes.

'Who are you? What are you doing here?'

'Er… my name is Herbert…'

'Herbert?' sneered the big mouse. 'Herbert? What sort of name is that for a mouse, then? Nobody's called Herbert in Bethlehem, are they!' In the gloom Herbert could see other mice behind the one who was speaking. 'So what do you think you're doing on our territory?'

'Am I? Oh, sorry. You see, I live in the co… no, it's too long a tale…'

'You trying to be funny, mate? Too long a tail?' growled another mouse whose tail was very long indeed.

'Not at all, not at all. And I'm sorry I'm on your land. I sheltered here from a huge cat…'

'Oh yeah – likely one,' sneered a third mouse. 'Well – you've got to go!'

'Or we'll make sure you go… get my message?' added the leader.

Before Herbert could open his mouth to ask them to let him stay, the stable doors opened and light flooded in.

'Freeze!' hissed the leader. 'Not a sound. Amber alert!'

All the mice were happy to obey except Herbert, who thought that it might be a good moment to escape. Quickly he scampered off along the floor, using the hay for cover. He reached a huge block of wood and began to climb it carefully. The hay no longer hid him, but he climbed into the roof space and stopped in the shadows, looking down on the scene below.

Two men were talking. Both of them were looking at the pile of hay and the younger man was nodding. After a few

moments he left the yard and the other one picked up a pitchfork and dug the prongs into the hay, spreading it all over the floor.

'Mice!' he roared and began to race around the stable chasing the gang of mice Herbert had met. Eyes popping out of their heads the gang scattered in every direction, yelling at the tops of their voices. Herbert kept still.

Satisfied at last with the hay, the man turned just as the young man entered the yard, this time with a woman. They talked a bit and then the man put down his bags and unfolded a blanket on the hay. The woman lay down on it. Another woman came into the stable and the two men left.

Herbert lost interest. He was hungry and he thought he was probably the only mouse left in the stable so… he tiptoed down to the floor and began to crawl inside the man's bag. You see – he hadn't learned a thing! With a squeal of pleasure he found a piece of cheese which he carried in his teeth back up to his perch high above. What he saw then almost made him drop the chunk of cheese. Below him, the woman on the blanket had produced a baby human which began to make a dreadful noise. 'Thank goodness baby mice don't squeak so much,' he thought.

Herbert watched, but no more baby humans were born. He watched as the other woman wrapped the baby and put it in a feeding trough. 'Pity,' thought Herbert, 'I was going to check that out for food later.' The woman on the blanket rested and then the young man came in and made all sorts of 'coochy-coo' noises over the baby. 'Yuk,' said Herbert under his breath.

All was peaceful for half an hour or so and then there was a noise at the stable gates. The older man opened the gates and a group of other men came in. Herbert knew they were shepherds because he'd spent a

© **pfp** publishing limited 2002 ISBN 1 874050 59 7 May be photocopied for use only within the purchasing institution **pfp**, 61 Gray's Inn Road, London WC1X 8TH

64

lifetime eating their lunches! He watched while they kneeled down around the baby human. One of them held out a lamb which the young man took and put at the baby's feet.

Herbert looked at the baby which was looking up towards the roof. It looked as though he was looking straight at Herbert, who waved a paw very carefully in case he was seen. The human baby didn't seem to get the idea though – it didn't wave back.

The men went and after washing the mother's face even the other woman left as well. The mother closed her eyes and slept.

Herbert was confused. He had a feeling that this was a special baby, and that he ought to give the baby a present like the shepherds had done, but he didn't know what he could give it.

Then Herbert had an idea. Picking up the piece of cheese in his mouth he climbed down again, crossed the floor and climbed up the leg of the manger – the feeding trough. He found himself staring again into the baby's eyes, this time at very close range. The baby gurgled and smiled and Herbert almost fainted, until he realised that he wasn't being threatened. Slowly he placed the piece of cheese beside the baby's head and placed a paw on his shoulder before turning to scramble back down to the ground.

As he reached his perch he heard people entering again. If he could have understood human talk he'd have heard the young man say, 'Now how on earth did this piece of cheese get here?' But of course, he couldn't.

Conclusion

Herbert felt that something special had happened that night, and he was right. The baby born in the stable was Jesus. It was the first Christmas and the lamb brought by the shepherds was the first Christmas present, given to celebrate the birth of Jesus.

Herbert wanted to do the same as them to mark the special occasion and now we give presents to each other at Christmas because of what happened on that night.

No doubt Herbert had a lovely story to tell when, at last, he made his way back into the countryside and left Bethlehem to the town mice who lived there.

Prayer

Thank you Lord for the wonderful birth of Jesus. Thank you for sending the shepherds to be the first people to visit the Son of God. We know that Jesus was born for all of us – rich and poor. Help us to be good people, just like him. Amen.

Thought

Christmas is a wonderful time with lots of fun and happiness. Let's try to be really happy people throughout Christmas, so that everyone who meets us has a little bit of our happiness rub off onto them.

Carol

'Away in a Manger'

Assemblies

Could it happen today?

This assembly is light-hearted and hopefully thought-provoking. It places Christmas in a modern setting and provides characters who parallel those in the Christmas story.

Introduction

We always look back when we read the Christmas story. After all, it happened over two thousand years ago. It couldn't happen today – could it? Well, listen to this story and see what you think.

Story

The town was stuffed full of people. They'd come from all over the place for several different reasons. First, there was the Cup Final, then the annual conference of the teachers' union, and as if that wasn't enough, the new exhibition centre had just opened. Take it from me – the town was full, which created a lot of problems for Joe and Mary when they turned up late in their battered old van.

They tried everywhere, but there wasn't a single spare room in any of the B&Bs or hotels. Even the local caravan park was full to bursting.

They had a problem. Mary was heavily pregnant and the baby was due almost any minute! Finding shelter was important. There was a local hospital, of course, but they wouldn't admit Mary until she'd shown the birth was about to begin, so they had to find somewhere for the night.

They sat in the van, both thinking hard. The van wasn't an option!

'Got it!' yelled Joe, thumping the steering wheel. 'Remember my cousin Angus? Doesn't he live around here?'

'Don't know,' Mary sighed. 'Oh, Joe – we've got to find somewhere.'

'Yeah, that's what I'm saying. He lives here somewhere. Wait a minute.'

Joe fished in his pocket and took out a mobile. He phoned his uncle and got the address of this long-lost cousin Angus. 'Right – it's worth a try,' he said as the van rattled off down the road. Mary was asleep, tired by the journey, which was just as well.

Cousin Angus could only vaguely recall Joe but he seemed friendly enough. They didn't have any room though. Their house was already full of visiting football fans so…

'You're our last hope. Really. We'll sleep anywhere,' pleaded Joe.

'Look, about the only free space we've got is the garage…' began Angus, deliberately being light-hearted.

'Yes! Great!' replied Joe enthusiastically. 'We'll take it. I've got some rugs in the van…'

'Hey – steady on – I was only joking,' said Angus.

'But I'm not,' countered Joe. 'If you're prepared to have us in your garage we'll be very grateful.'

'Well, OK then. We've got lilos, pillows and blankets galore. There's a heater too, which I can plug in. Goodness knows what Doris will have to say…'

In case Angus changed his mind when he spoke to his wife, Joe leaped into the van and reversed it up to the garage. He helped Mary out and together they entered the garage. Doris came in and was very worried at the thought of a pregnant woman sleeping in her garage, but did everything she could to make the place cosy.

Assemblies ☆

☆Could it happen today?

At last it was ready and Mary lay down gratefully to rest. The plan was that in the morning Mary would be driven to the local hospital if necessary, but nature has a funny way of organising its own timetable. Mary went into labour shortly after lying down. There wasn't time to get to hospital so Doris rolled up her sleeves and made Joe and Angus find boiling water and clean towels.

A baby boy was born some time later in the middle of the night. Doris wrapped him in towels and searched frantically for somewhere to put him down for a moment. Her eye caught sight of Angus's tool box lying beside the Ford Escort which occupied most of the space. 'That'll do nicely,' she thought and pulled it nearer. Grabbing most of the tools she put them on the floor, covered the metal edges of the toolbox with a blanket and lay the baby down. Now she could look after Mary.

Later on, Mary, Joe, Doris and Angus were looking down at the baby, who still lay in the toolbox.

'What are you going to call him?' asked Angus.

'Jesus,' replied Mary with conviction.

'Jesus? That's an unusual name,' said Doris.

'Yes, but he's a special baby, you see,' Mary explained.

Just then there was a hesitant rap on the metal garage door. Angus opened it to reveal three men.

'Excuse me,' said one. 'This is going to sound really daft but – is there a new baby here? Only we were told to come into town and find him.'

'Come in,' invited Angus. 'It's not as silly as it sounds. He's here.'

The visitors – who explained that they were farmers who lived about six miles away – kneeled down around the baby for a while before standing. One of them put a box on the floor. 'We thought we'd bring a few organic vegetables for you. We couldn't come empty handed!' he joked.

The farmers thanked Angus and Doris for letting them in and one of them said, 'I can't really explain it. We were leaning on a gate at the time, checking for badgers. Something happened which we can't really understand, even now. We heard voices, saw lights… Well, we thought we were seeing things, but we all saw and heard the same things. So we got in the Range Rover and came over.' Still confused but now excited as well, they went on their way.

It was almost dawn and the other guests – who had slept soundly through all the excitement – were due to leave early.

'Right – we are all moving into the house now,' declared Doris. 'I'm not having Mary and Jesus in this garage a moment longer. Angus, wake up those lazy lads and tell them breakfast's cooking and I want the room back!'

It was all hustle and bustle but within a couple of hours Mary and Jesus were in a warm bed with fresh sheets and Doris was in her element organising everyone. Joe was sent off to buy nappies and baby clothes while Angus went off to work happy to escape!

For several days nothing unusual happened. The doctor came to see Mary and pronounced her fighting fit and the baby very healthy. Lots of cups of tea, sleep, a bit of TV and the odd jam doughnut had done wonders for Mary.

And then the front doorbell rang. On the doorstep stood three people – two men and a woman. They apologised for arriving without telephoning but said that they hadn't known where they were going until they got there! This was all a bit too confusing for Doris but she let them in when they asked if there was a new and very important baby inside.

Assemblies

☆Could it happen today?

'Of course he's very important, the little cherub,' said Doris as she ushered them in. 'Have you come far?' she asked.

'Oh yes,' said the lady. 'We all landed at Heathrow today. Sorry, I should explain. We are all... professors, I suppose you might say. We carry out research in our countries.'

'Well,' interrupted one of the men excitedly, 'we all began to realise that something great was about to happen here, in your country. A baby was to be born who would become very, very important to the world.'

'So,' began the third, 'we spoke to each other on the phone – and hopped on a plane and – here we are.'

'I see...' said Doris, who plainly didn't.

'I understand,' called Mary from the bedroom. 'Please come in.' They all trooped in and stood around the cot that Joe had bought. Each of them gently put down a gift for the new baby on the bed and made all the usual noises people make when they meet a baby.

'Of course,' began the lady, 'we visited your Prime Minister at No. 10 Downing Street first. He seemed amazed that a world leader had been born and wanted to know more. He thought we were crazy when we told him we were following a star!'

'A star?' asked Doris.

'Well, a satellite anyway!' answered one of the men. 'And now we must go. Thank you for letting us in. Goodbye.' They all shook hands and the three wise people went back to their taxi, which was waiting for them by the pavement.

Conclusion

Well, does the story work in modern times? Could it happen like that? What did you think? (*Take responses.*)

Thank you. You must confess though, that the story was different. Something to think about. Maybe it's something to write about in class. Would you have known what to do if you were Joe? Would you have let people sleep in your garage? Would you have jumped on a plane to Heathrow? What would you think if all those strangers turned up at your house?

When you get home tonight just think. These amazing things happened to ordinary people like us.

Prayer

Dear Lord, when you were born your family were ordinary people living in an ordinary way. It was your birth which made everything extraordinary. Help us to learn from the story we have heard. Help us to ask ourselves how we would have greeted you if you came to Earth today. Amen.

Thought

We are told that Jesus was born in a stable, not in a palace. This is because He came among ordinary people at a time when anyone who was 'educated' lived in a palace. Very few people in those days had any education. Let's be glad that we live at a time and in a country where everyone has the chance of gaining a good education. We must try not to waste the opportunities we have.

Carol

'Once in Royal David's City'

Assemblies ✪

68

Jesus's birthday

Alan Biddle

1. Sing lul - la - by to ba - by Je - sus
2. Ring out the bells for Je - sus - 's birth - day

Watch o - ver him a - sleep in the hay.
Let us be glad for God's on - ly son.

Jesus's birthday ⭐ **Carols and songs**

Sing lullaby to baby Jesus
Watch over him asleep in the hay.
Sing lullaby dear Mary is resting
Tired from the travelling during the day.

Ring out the bells for Jesus's birthday
Let us be glad for God's only son.
Ring out the bells and spread the good tidings
Jesus is born for ev'ry one.

Carols and songs ★ *Jesus's birthday*

Travellers

Alan Biddle

Travellers ⭐ **Carols and songs**

Carols and songs ⭐ *Travellers*

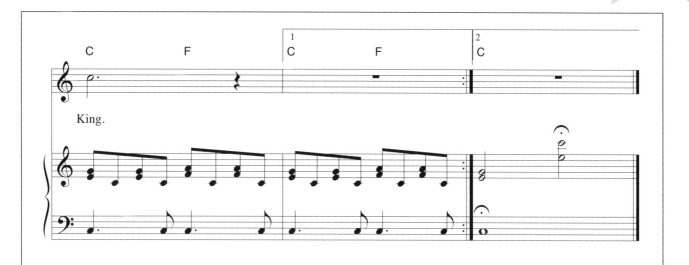

King.

We are on a journey, a journey from afar.
We have followed closely a brightly shining star.
With faces lifted up to see its glory in the night.
Only his tender love for us could ever shine so bright.

Chorus
Allelu Alleluya
Let all God's children sing.
Allelu Alleluya
Sing praises to our King.

We stopped at a stable and quietly inside
Lay a babe so safe and warm, to look at him we tried.
We left our gifts and worshipped this small and precious boy.
Join in our song of praise to show our wonder and our joy.

Allelu Alleluya
Let all God's children sing.
Allelu Alleluya
Sing praises to our King.

Travellers ★ Carols and songs

© **pfp** publishing limited 2002 ISBN 1 874050 59 7 May be photocopied for use only within the purchasing institution **pfp**, 61 Gray's Inn Road, London WC1X 8TH

Show us the way

Alan Biddle

© **pfp** publishing limited 2002 ISBN 1 874050 59 7 May be photocopied for use only within the purchasing institution **pfp**, 61 Gray's Inn Road, London WC1X 8TH **pfp**

Show us the way ⭐ **Carols and songs**

Show us the way at Christmas
To follow the Lord's shining star.
Show us the way at Christmas
As we travel so near from afar.
Show us the way at Christmas
To offer the baby our love.
Show us the way at Christmas
To our Lord in heaven above.

Show us the way as onward
We travel the road with His news.
Show us the way tomorrow
To live by His word as we choose.
Show us the way each moment
To ask for His presence within.
Show us the way forever
To grow ever closer to Him.

Carols and songs ★ *Show us the way*

Child Jesus

Alan Biddle

Child Jesus ★ **Carols and songs**

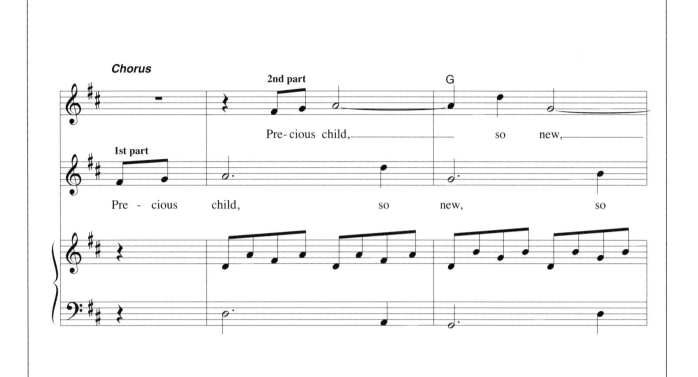

Child Jesus ⭐ Carols and songs

page 11 of 36

on earth ——— to give us heav'n-ly grace.

earth a sac - ri - fice to give us heav'n-ly grace.

If I come nearby a tiny child, new born, asleep on hay
How can I know that he will be for me, the only way?
A child so small, one day will be a man for sinners slain
And as I look upon his face, the beauty causes pain.

Chorus
Precious child, so new, so small, with starlight in your face.
Your life on earth a sacrifice to give us heav'nly grace.

Your tiny hand fits into mine, yet you are Christ the Lord,
Son of God and King of Kings, the Father's only word.
I will come nearby that tiny child and ask him to forgive.
Because he died upon my cross, with him I know I live.

Precious child, so new, so small, with starlight in your face.
Your life on earth a sacrifice to give us heav'nly grace.

*(The third time you can can combine the chorus sung in two parts
with a small group singing the verse to 'La'.)*

Carols and songs ★ *Child Jesus*

A gift for Christmas

Alan Biddle

A gift for Christmas ⭐ Carols and songs

page 13 of 36

Carols and songs ★ *A gift for Christmas*

82

Small is my gift, small is my life
Jesus I love to be by your side.
Here is my gift, living for you.
Take all I have, your word is true.

Small is my gift, small is my life
Jesus I give to others in strife.
Torn is the world, crying in pain.
Gently I come, your life to gain.

Large is your gift, large is your life.
Jesus you show us wrong from right.
Teaching us how to live in peace.
Giving your life that wars may cease.

I have a gift, special and true,
To love one another as I love you.

A gift for Christmas ★ **Carols and songs**

A Christmas party

Alan Biddle

Carols and songs ✪ *A Christmas party*

birth of a boy.___ Bring all your friends and fam-'ly___

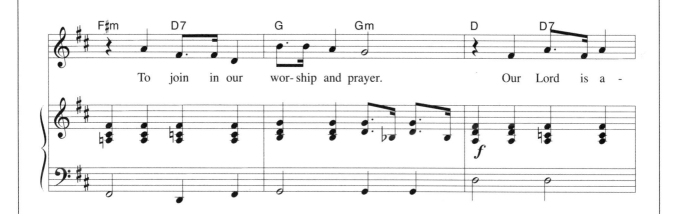

To join in our wor-ship and prayer. Our Lord is a -

live at Christ-mas So ce-le-brate.___ he'll be there.___

A Christmas party ★ **Carols and songs**

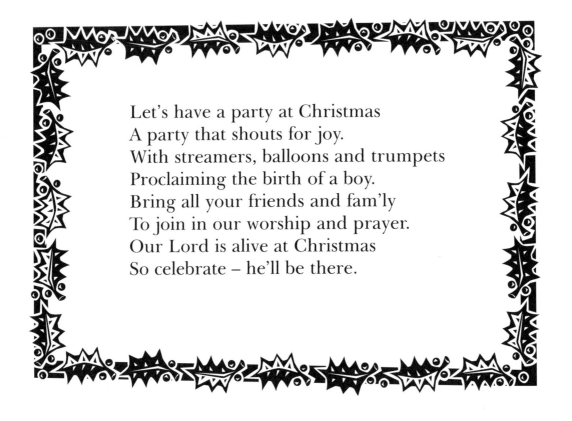

Let's have a party at Christmas
A party that shouts for joy.
With streamers, balloons and trumpets
Proclaiming the birth of a boy.
Bring all your friends and fam'ly
To join in our worship and prayer.
Our Lord is alive at Christmas
So celebrate – he'll be there.

Carols and songs ★ *A Christmas party*

Sing Alleluia

Jim Fox

Sing Alleluia ★ **Carols and songs**

© **pfp** publishing limited 2002 ISBN 1 874050 59 7 May be photocopied for use only within the purchasing institution **pfp**, 61 Gray's Inn Road, London WC1X 8TH

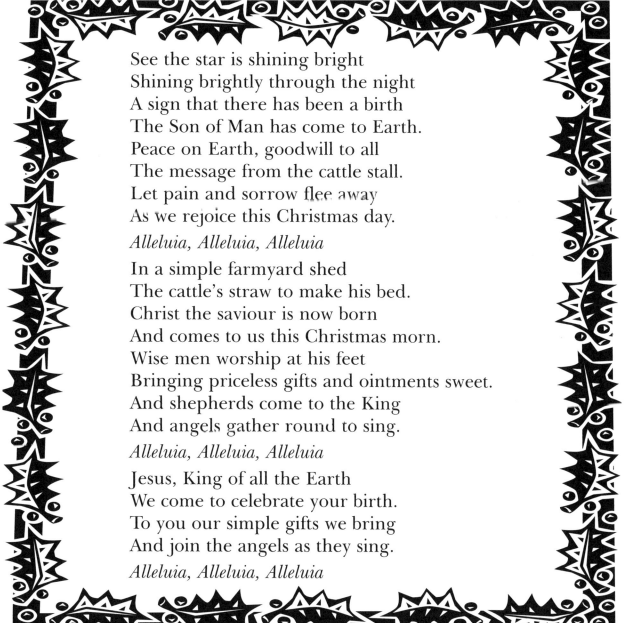

See the star is shining bright
Shining brightly through the night
A sign that there has been a birth
The Son of Man has come to Earth.
Peace on Earth, goodwill to all
The message from the cattle stall.
Let pain and sorrow flee away
As we rejoice this Christmas day.

Alleluia, Alleluia, Alleluia

In a simple farmyard shed
The cattle's straw to make his bed.
Christ the saviour is now born
And comes to us this Christmas morn.
Wise men worship at his feet
Bringing priceless gifts and ointments sweet.
And shepherds come to the King
And angels gather round to sing.

Alleluia, Alleluia, Alleluia

Jesus, King of all the Earth
We come to celebrate your birth.
To you our simple gifts we bring
And join the angels as they sing.

Alleluia, Alleluia, Alleluia

Sing Alleluia ★ **Carols and songs**

Ring out the bells

Jim Fox

Sing a song of free-dom ev'-ry girl and boy at the chan-ging of the sea-son we'll sing a song of joy. Mid-

Ring out the bells ⭐ **Carols and songs**

Carols and songs ⭐ *Ring out the bells*

winter has come u - p - on us   it's the
turn - ing   of   the   year   bring - ing
hope   and   joy   to   ev' ry heart   and
wi - ping a - way   all   tears   it's the

Ring out the bells ✪ **Carols and songs**

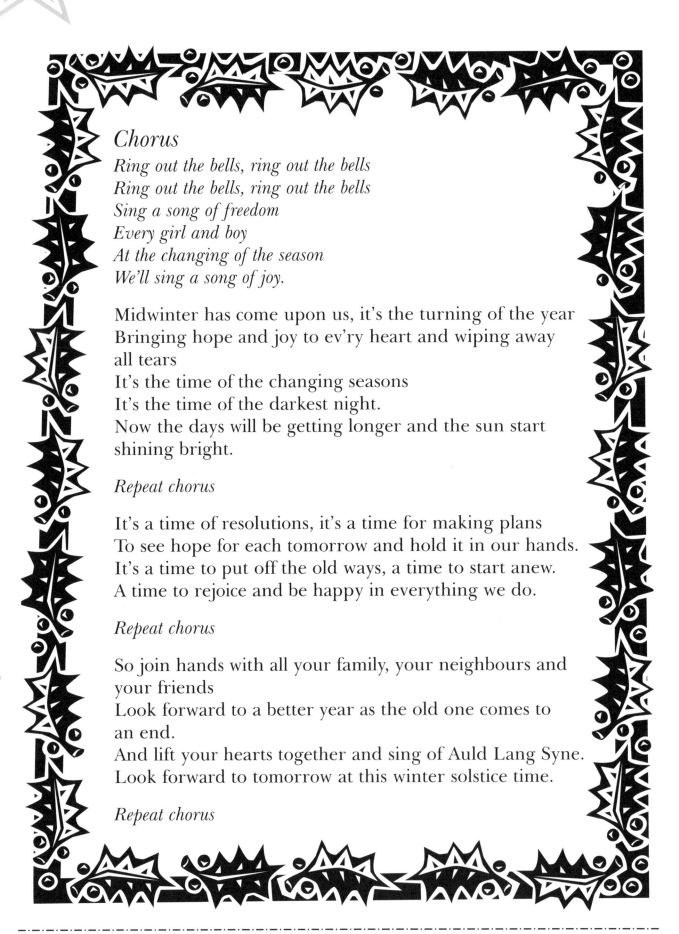

Chorus

Ring out the bells, ring out the bells
Ring out the bells, ring out the bells
Sing a song of freedom
Every girl and boy
At the changing of the season
We'll sing a song of joy.

Midwinter has come upon us, it's the turning of the year
Bringing hope and joy to ev'ry heart and wiping away
all tears
It's the time of the changing seasons
It's the time of the darkest night.
Now the days will be getting longer and the sun start
shining bright.

Repeat chorus

It's a time of resolutions, it's a time for making plans
To see hope for each tomorrow and hold it in our hands.
It's a time to put off the old ways, a time to start anew.
A time to rejoice and be happy in everything we do.

Repeat chorus

So join hands with all your family, your neighbours and
your friends
Look forward to a better year as the old one comes to
an end.
And lift your hearts together and sing of Auld Lang Syne.
Look forward to tomorrow at this winter solstice time.

Repeat chorus

Carols and songs ✪ *Ring out the bells*

The snowman's song

Jim Fox

The snowman's song ★ **Carols and songs**

Carols and songs ☆ *The snowman's song*

not ve - ry long since I came in - to being but my

eyes find it hard to be - lieve what they're seeing. Now you're

prob - ab - ly wond'ring why I'm stan - ding here whining you see

I'm a poor snow - man and the sun's

The snowman's song ✪ **Carols and songs**

Carols and songs ★ *The snowman's song*

98

It's not very long since I came into being
But my eyes find it hard to believe what they're seeing.
Now you're probably wond'ring why I'm standing here whining
You see, I'm a poor snowman and the sun's started shining.

Chorus

Being a snowman isn't much fun
When you wake up on Boxing Day to be greeted by the sun.
I can't begin to tell you just how I felt
When I looked down at my feet
And they started to melt.

My nose started running and so did my hand.
When your legs turn to slush it's not easy to stand.
I'm feeling very sad now but people say I oughta
Pull myself together, but it's not easy when you're turning to water.

Repeat chorus

Now time's running out and soon I'll be no more.
Just a pile of old clothes in a heap on the floor.
You might think I'm a moaner but my life is in a muddle
And it's hard to keep on smiling when you find you're just a puddle.

Repeat chorus

The snowman's song ✪ **Carols and songs**

© **pfp** publishing limited 2002 ISBN 1 874050 59 7 May be photocopied for use only within the purchasing institution **pfp**, 61 Gray's Inn Road, London WC1X 8TH

Christmas Day

Jim Fox

seven o - clock on Christmas day and I'm sitting on the end of my bed the

It's

© **pfp** publishing limited 2002 ISBN 1 874050 59 7 May be photocopied for use only within the purchasing institution **pfp**, 61 Gray's Inn Road, London WC1X 8TH

Carols and songs ⭐ *Christmas Day*

Christmas Day ✪ Carols and songs

Last verse: repeat chorus after 𝄋 and then:

Christmas Day ★ **Carols and songs**

It's 7 o'clock on Christmas Day and I'm sitting on the end of my bed.
The wrapping paper is piling high, it's nearly up to my head.
I've got lots of presents from all my friends and all my family
And when I get downstairs I'm sure I'll find some more stuck under the tree.
I've got a computer game and a colouring book, an orange and a music box.
I've got a magic set and a racing car and 14 pairs of socks,
Some modelling clay and a talking bear and a money box with a key
And when I get downstairs I'm sure I'll find some more stuff under the tree.

Chorus
And Auntie's sat in the corner, sipping a glass of sherry
And you can bet your life she'll still be there
When the Queen comes on the telly.

It's 1 o'clock and we're sitting down to the traditional Christmas dinner.
And by the time we've got through all this food we won't be any thinner.
My plate is piled up really high and Mum says if I'm good
And eat up all of my dinner I can have some Christmas pud.
We've got turkey, peas, carrots and beans, parsnips and cranberry sauce.
We've got roast potatoes and mashed ones too and that's just the first course.
We've got sage and onion stuffing, and it all tastes really good
And when I've eaten all my dinner I can have some Christmas pud.

Chorus

Now it's 3 o'clock and we gather round to watch the Queen's speech on the telly.
There's me and Mum and Dad and John and even Auntie Nelly.
Then later on in the afternoon we get the chocolates out.
And I think by the time I go to bed I'll be ill without a doubt.
There are strawberry cremes and caramels and ones with nutty centres,
Hazlenut Whirls and Turkish delight that Uncle Ernie sent us.
And when it's time to go to bed I'll be feeling a little bit ill.
But not as bad as Auntie, who's in the corner still.

Yes Auntie's still in the corner with another glass of sherry
And by the look on her face I think that she
Is more than a little bit merry.

Repeat final chorus

Notes for teachers

The literacy and numeracy worksheets on pages 110–151 have been designed to address specific objectives in the National Literacy and Numeracy Strategies. Other worksheets are linked to the relevant sections of the National Curriculum.

The objectives are listed here along with the intended age group. Ages are not indicated on the worksheets to make it easier for you to use the sheets with a variety of children.

Literacy

1   YR Word level work: Phonological awareness, phonics and spelling 2 knowledge of grapheme/phoneme correspondences through: hearing and identifying initial sounds on words; reading letter(s) that represent(s) the sound(s) a-z, ch, sh, th; writing each letter in response to each sound.

2   YR Text level work: Reading comprehension 7 to use knowledge of familiar texts to re-enact or re-tell to others, recounting the main points in correct sequence.

3   YR Text level work: Composition 12 through guided and independent writing: to experiment with writing in a variety of play, exploratory and role-play situations; to write their own names; to write labels or captions for pictures and drawings; to write sentences or match pictures or sequences of pictures; to experiment with writing and recognise how their own

version matches and differs from conventional version...

4   Y1T1 Text level work: Reading comprehension 13 to read and follow simple instructions... **Writing composition 16** to write and draw simple instructions and labels for everyday classroom use.

5   Y1T1 Sentence level work: Sentence construction and punctuation 5 to recognise full stops and capital letters when reading and name them correctly; **7** that a line of writing is not necessarily a sentence; **8** to begin using full stops to demarcate sentences; **9** to use a capital letter for the personal pronoun 'I' and for the start of a sentence.

6   Y1T1 Sentence level work: Grammatical awareness 1 to expect written text to make sense and to check for sense if it does not; **4** to write captions and simple sentences, and to re-read, recognising whether or not they make sense, e.g. missing words, wrong word order.

7   Y2T1 Text level work: Reading comprehension 4 to understand time and sequential relationships in stories, ie. what happened when.

8   Y2T1 Sentence level work: Grammatical awareness 2 to find examples, in fiction and non-fiction, of words and phrases that link sentences, eg. after, meanwhile, during, before, then, next, after a while.

● **Worksheets**

Worksheets ✪

9 Y2T1 Sentence level work: Sentence construction and punctuation 5 to revise knowledge about other uses of capitalisation, e.g. for names, headings, titles, emphasis, and begin to use in own writing.

10 Y3T1 Sentence level work: Sentence construction and punctuation 7 the basic conventions of speech punctuation through: identifying speech marks in reading; beginning to use in own writing; using capital letters to mark the start of direct speech; **8** to use the term 'speech marks'.

11 Y3T1 Sentence level work: Sentence construction and punctuation 6 to secure knowledge of question marks and exclamation marks in reading, understand their purpose and use appropriately in own writing.

12 Y3T1 Sentence level work: Grammatical awareness 3 the function of verbs in sentences through: noticing that sentences cannot make sense without them; collecting and classifying examples of verbs from reading and own knowledge... experimenting with changing simple verbs in sentences and discussing their impact on meaning.

13 Y4T1 Text level work: Writing composition 11 to write character sketches, focusing on small details to evoke sympathy or dislike.

14 Y4T1 Sentence level work: Grammatical awareness 2 to revise work on verbs from Year 1 term 3 and to investigate verb tenses (past, present and future)...

15 Y4T1 Sentence level work: Grammatical awareness 3 to identify the use of powerful verbs eg. 'hobbled' instead of 'went', e.g. through cloze procedure.

16 Y5T1 Text level work: Writing composition 25 to write instructional texts, and test them out, eg. instructions for loading computers, design briefs for technology, rules for games.

17 and 18 Y5T1 Sentence level work: Grammatical awareness 1 to investigate word order by examining how far the order of words in sentences can be changed: which words are essential to meaning; which can be deleted without damaging the basic meaning; which words or groups of words can be moved into a different order.

19 Y6T1 Sentence level work: Grammatical awareness 1 to revise from Y5 the different word classes, e.g. prepositions.

20 Y6T1 Text level work: Writing composition 9 to prepare a short section of story as a script, e.g. using stage directions, location/setting.

21. Y6T1 Text level work: Writing composition 15 to develop a journalistic style through considering: balanced and ethical reporting; what is of public interest in events; the interest of the reader; selection and presentation of information.

☆Learning objectives

Numeracy

1 YR Adding and subtracting 14 begin to relate addition to combining two groups of objects, counting all the objects; extend to three groups of objects.

2 YR Solving problems 18 solve simple problems or puzzles in a practical context and respond to 'what could we try next?' **19** Sort and match objects, pictures or children themselves, justifying the decisions made.

3 YR Measures, shape and space 27 use everyday words to describe position, direction and movement: for example, follow and give instructions about positions, directions and movements in PE and other activities.

4 Y1 Solving problems 90, 92 solve a given problem by sorting, classifying and organising information in simple ways, such as: using objects or pictures; in a list or simple table. Discuss and explain results.

5 Y1 Numbers and the number system 16 understand and use the vocabulary of estimation. Give a sensible estimate of a number of objects that can be checked by counting (e.g. up to about 30 objects).

6 Y1 Calculations 30 know by heart: all pairs of numbers with a total of 10; addition facts for all pairs of numbers with a total up to at least 5 and the corresponding subtraction facts; addition doubles of all numbers to at least 5. Begin to know: addition facts for all pairs of numbers with a total up to at least 10 and the corresponding subtraction facts.

7 Y2 Solving problems 91, 93 solve a given problem by sorting, classifying and organising information in simple ways such as: in a list or simple table; in a pictogram; in a block graph. Discuss and explain results.

8 Y2 Measures, shape and space 87, 89 recognise whole, half and quarter turns, to the left or right, clockwise or anti-clockwise. Know that a right-angle is a measure of a quarter turn, and recognise right-angles in squares and rectangles. Give instructions for moving along a route in straight lines and round right-angled corners; for example, to pass through a simple maze.

9 Y2 Calculations 53 know by heart: multiplication facts for the 2 and 10 times tables; doubles of all numbers to 10 and the corresponding halves. Begin to know: multiplication facts for the 5 times table.

10 Y3 Measures, shape and space 87 recognise and use the four compass directions N, S, E and W. **89** Make and describe right-angled turns, including turns between the four compass points.

11 Y3 Numbers and the number system 17 Read and begin to write the vocabulary of estimation and approximation. Give a sensible estimate of up to about 100 objects. **19** Round any 2 digit number to the nearest 10 and any 3 digit number to the nearest 100.

12 Y3 Numbers and the number system 21, 23 recognise unit fractions … and use them to find fractions of shapes and numbers. Begin to recognise simple fractions that are several parts of a whole… Begin to recognise simple equivalent fractions… Compare familiar fractions… Estimate a simple fraction.

✪ Worksheets

13 Y4 Solving problems 82–89 use all four operations to solve word problems involving numbers in real life, money and measures (including time), using one or more steps, including converting pounds to pence and metres to centimetres and vice versa.

14 Y4 Numbers and the number system 22 use fraction notation. Recognise simple fractions that are several parts of a whole...and mixed numbers... recognise the equivalence of simple fractions... Order simple fractions... **24** Begin to relate fractions to division and find simple fractions.

15 Y4 Handling data 114, 116 solve a problem by collecting quickly, organising, representing and interpreting data in tables charts, graphs and diagrams, including those generated by a computer.

16 Y5 Calculations 41 find differences by counting up through next multiple of 10, 100 or 1000... Partition into H, T and U, adding the most significant digits first. Identify near doubles... Add or subtract the nearest multiple of 10 or 100, then adjust. **43** Develop further the relationship between + and -. Add several numbers. **45, 47** Use known number facts and place value for mental addition and subtraction.

17 Y5 Handling data 115, 117 solve a problem by representing and interpreting data in tables, charts, graphs and diagrams, including those generated by a computer... Find the mode of a set of data.

18 Y5 Solving problems 75 choose and use appropriate number operations to solve problems, and appropriate ways of calculating: mental, mental with jottings, written methods, calculator.

19 Y6 Solving problems 82–89 identify and use appropriate operations (including combinations of operations) to solve problems involving numbers and quantities... Explain methods and reasoning.

20 Y6 Numbers and the number system 33 understand percentage as the number of parts in every 100. Express simple fractions ... as percentages. Find simple percentages of small whole-number quantities.

21 Y6 Measures, shape and space 105 make shapes with increasing accuracy. Visualise 3-D shapes from 2-D drawings and identify different nets for a closed cube.

Science

Key Stage 1

1   Sc1: Scientific Enquiry: 1, 2a–c,g–j
       Sc4: Physical Processes: 1a–c
       Links: Eng 1/1c,3c, 1/10, 2/7a,7b, 3/1d,1e; Ma 2/5a,5b; ICT 3

2   Sc1: Scientific Enquiry: 2a–d,g–j
       Sc3: Materials and their properties: 1b,c,d
       Links: Eng 1/1c, 1/10, 2/7a,7b, 3c, 3/1d,1e; Ma 2/5a,5b; ICT 3

3   Sc1: Scientific enquiry: 1, 2a–d, e–j
       Sc3: Materials and their properties: 1a,b
       Links: En 1/10, 2/7a,7b, 1/1c,3c, 3/1d,1e; Ma 2/5a,b; ICT 3

4   Sc1: Scientific Enquiry: 1, 2a,b,g,h,j
       Sc2: Life processes and living things: 1c, 2b,c,e,g

Worksheets ✪

☆Learning objectives

5 Sc1: Scientific Enquiry: 1, 2a–d,e–g,h–j
Sc2: Materials and their properties
1a,b,c,d, 2a
Links: En 1/1c,3c, 1/10, 2/7a,7b, 3/1d,1e;
Ma 3/4a,4c; ICT sorting materials

6 Sc1: Scientific Enquiry: 1, 2[a,b,e,f,g,h,i,j
Sc2: Life processes and living things: 1b,
2b,c,d
Links: En 1/1c,3c, 1/10, 2/7a,7b, 3/1d,1e;
Ma 3/4a,4c

Key Stage 2

7 Sc1: Scientific Enquiry 1a,b, 2a–m
Sc3: Materials and their properties: 1a
Links to: ICT 2h/3; Eng 1/10, 2/3; Ma
2/2i, 3/4a,4b

8 Sc1: Scientific Enquiry: 2a,b,h,i,j,k
Sc2: Life processes and living things:
1a,c, 2a,b, 4a,b,c
Links to: Eng 1/10, 2/3; Ma 2/2I, 4a,4d;
ICT database

9 Sc1: Scientific Enquiry: 1a,b 2a–m
Sc3: Materials and their properties:
1a,e, 2b,d,f,g
Links to: Eng1/10, 2/3; Ma 3/4a,4b; ICT
2b, 3

10 Sc1: Scientific Enquiry: 1a,b,
2a,b,c,f,h,I,j,k,l,m
Sc2: Life Processes and living things:
1b,c
Sc3: Materials and their properties: 1a,
2b,d,f,g
Links: Eng 1/10, 2/3; Ma3, 4a,4b; ICT
2b/3

11 Sc1: Scientific Enquiry: 1a,b, 2a–m
Sc3: Materials and their properties:
3a–e
Links: Eng1/10, 2/3; Ma 2/2I, 3/4a,b;
ICT 2b/3

12 Sc1: Scientific Enquiry: 1a,
2a,b,c,e,f,h,i,j,k,l,m
Sc2: Life Processes and living things: 1a,
2a,b,g,h
Links: En 1/10, 2/3; Ma 2/2I, 3/4a,4b,4d,
4/2; ICT 2b/3, + food analysis

13 Sc1: Scientific Enquiry: 1a, 2a,b,h,m
Sc2: Life processes and living things: 1a,
2a,b,g,h
Links: En 1/10, 2/3; ICT 3

14 Sc1: Scientific Enquiry: 1a,b, 2a–d,
e,j–m
Sc3: Materials and their properties: 1c
Sc4: Physical processes: 1a–c
Links: Eng 1/10, 2/3; Ma 3/4a,4b; ICT
simulated circuits; DT table decorations

Geography

All the worksheets address these
knowledge, skills and understanding:

KS1: 1a–d, 2a,c,d, 3a,b,d,e, 6b

KS2: 1a–c,e, 2a,c,d,f,g, 3a–c,f,g, 7b

Worksheets

Christmas words

Say the first sound of each picture. Now, write the sound at the start of the word next to the picture.

a  angel

b  baby

c  cracker

p  present

r  reindeer

s  shepherd

s  star

Santa's story

Look at this story. It's in the wrong order. Cut it out,
put it in the right order and tell it to a friend.

Worksheets

Missing words

These pictures tell a story. Write in the missing words.

Three Wise Men follow a _ _ _ _ _ .

The star stops over a small _ _ _ _ _ _ _ .

The Wise Men find a tiny _ _ _ _ _ .

They give him _ _ _ _ _ _ _ _ _ _ .

How to enjoy Christmas

Instructions tell you how to do things. Read the instructions for Christmas Morning then write your own instructions for pulling a cracker.

Instructions for Christmas Morning

1 Open your eyes and look for your stocking.

2 Zoom out of bed and grab your stocking.

3 Take care not to drop any presents.

4 Return to your warm bed.

5 Open all the presents by ripping the paper off.

6 Eat any chocolate before your big brother comes in.

7 Be happy and play with your new presents.

Instructions for pulling a cracker

1

2

3

☆ **Worksheets**

Christmas C.A.P.I.T.A.L.S.

Look at the sentences below. Find all the capital letters and put red circles round them. Find all the full stops and put green circles round them.

Christmas Day is wonderful.

I like giving people presents.

I hope Father Christmas comes to visit me.

Now look at these sentences. They all have mistakes. Find all the mistakes and put a red line under them.

i want to open my presents now.

We all go to church before we have presents

Mary and joseph found a stable

Now write three sentences about Christmas. Make sure they all start with a capital letter and end with a full stop.

1...

....

2...

....

3...

....

Worksheets ✪

© **pfp** publishing limited 2002 ISBN 1 874050 59 7 May be photocopied for use only within the purchasing institution **pfp**, 61 Gray's Inn Road, London WC1X 8TH **pfp**

Christmas missing words

All these sentences are missing a word. Choose the right one from the list under the sentence and write it in the space.

1 The Three Wise Men gave Jesus some _____.

chocolates   presents   flowers   rabbits

2 Father Christmas leaves presents in a _____.

dustbin    washing machine   tree   stocking

3 I like roast _____ for Christmas dinner.

cracker   socks   cabbage   turkey

4 Lots of people go to _____ to praise God.

London   church   cinemas   shops

5 I like Christmas _____ because they go bang.

puddings   crackers   cakes   trees

6 We decorate our _____ a week before Christmas.

tree   cooker   car   dog

☆ **Worksheets**

Topsy-turvy Christmas tales

The sentences in these Christmas stories are in the wrong order. Put numbers in the circles beside them to show which order they should be in.

◯ It stopped over a stable in Bethlehem.

◯ The Three Wise Men followed the star.

◯ They gave Jesus their gifts.

....

Did you get them in the right order? Now try these.

◯ Then I folded the paper over the ends of the present.

◯ First, I put the present in the middle of the paper.

◯ I stuck the paper down with sticky tape.

◯ Last of all I put a label on the present.

◯ She yawned, stretched and went to bed.

◯ Lucy wanted to see Father Christmas come down the chimney.

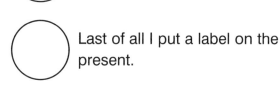

◯ After a while Lucy began to feel very sleepy.

◯ She hid behind the sofa and watched and listened.

....

On a new piece of paper, write out three or four sentences that make a story. Cut them out and jumble them up.

Now ask a friend to sort them out!

Worksheets ✪

Missing links

Write words in the spaces to link together the two parts of these sentences. Sometimes you need more than one word to make a whole sentence. There are lots of right answers.

Link words

Here are some words you could use to fill the spaces. Some of them fit more than once. You may be able to think of others.

while	even though
after	then
before	and
because	until

1 Nula wrote the cards _____ Thomas licked the envelopes.

2 Father Christmas sheltered from the rain under a tree _____ he went on his way around the houses.

3 Sita is sulking _____ she didn't get the present she wanted.

4 In our house, Dad does all the cooking _____ washes up.

5 I ate chocolate biscuits _____ I felt sick!

6 Father Christmas delivered all the presents _____ Mother Christmas got his breakfast ready.

7 I hung up my stocking _____ I went to bed.

8 Ali felt hungry _____ he had eaten a huge meal.

9 I felt all my presents _____ _____ I had been told not to.

10 My teacher fell over the Christmas tree _____ sitting down on a Christmas cake in the staff room!

☆ Worksheets

Christmas CAPITALS

Can you spot the mistakes in the sentence? Tell your partner. There are three mistakes!

my name is father christmas.

Look at these two lists. Write a capital letter in the space above each name.

People

joseph   herod

mary   balthazar   jesus

melchior   caspar

Places

bethlehem   jerusalem

nazareth

Find the words that need capital letters in these sentences. Write the letter in the space above the word.

1   the carol singers were very cold.

2   the christmas tree looked

beautiful.

3   After our christmas meal we all

went out to make a snowman.

4   mrs walker's class had a great

party at the end of term.

5   we all went shopping in london to

buy our christmas presents.

6   my cracker didn't go bang.

7   uncle bob and auntie jade came

over for boxing day.

8   i love christmas day!

Worksheets ✪

All you need for Christmas

"What did you say?"

Add speech marks to these sentences. Write them in the space above the words.

1 I want some more turkey please said Sunil.

2 Rudolph refuses to get up this morning said Father Christmas.

3 The carol service was a great success announced Mr Sims.

4 We will need some more potatoes for Christmas dinner.

These are a bit harder. Add speech marks and capital letters in the space above the words.

5 stop playing recorders while the choir is singing said Miss Crump.

6 a piece of holly in my sister's bed should sort her out said Ben.

7 let's sing the first carol on the sheet announced the vicar.

8 put this parcel in the bag over there ordered Father Christmas.

9 make sure you wrap up warmly dear fussed Mother Christmas.

10 the school parties will start after lunchtime declared Mr McMangler.

☆ **Worksheets**

All you need for Christmas

Ask me a question!

Look at each of these sentences. Some are questions, but beware – some are not! If it is a question, put a question mark in the circle. If it isn't, put a full stop.

1   Will Father Christmas be visiting

me this year ◯

2   Would you like to come to our

Christmas party ◯

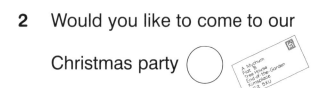

3   I want to wrap all the presents by

myself this year ◯

4   Are we going to church on

Christmas Day ◯

5   Did you get a joke in

your cracker ◯

6   There are only ten more

days until Christmas ◯

Some of these sentences are exclamations. If it is an exclamation, put an exclamation mark in the circle. If it isn't, put a full stop.

7   Look – Father Christmas is stuck

in that chimney ◯

8   The carol singers came

round last night ◯

9   When Grandma dropped

the pudding it broke the

floor tiles ◯

10 Quickly – the Christmas tree is

falling over ◯

11 We are going to visit Aunt Kate

before Christmas ◯

12 My baby brother yelled

so much that everyone

stopped singing ◯

Worksheets ✪

What we do at Christmas

Underline the verbs in each sentence. Try to think of better verbs to make the sentence more interesting.

1 I love Christmas cake.

2 We go to church on Christmas morning.

3 The best part of Christmas is giving presents to other people.

4 Father Christmas always drinks the milk I put by my bed for him.

Then underline the verbs in this passage. There are lots of them!

On Christmas Day lots of people go to church. Mrs Robson runs, Mr Sneep hobbles, Miss Smith wobbles, Colonel Crumpet marches, Mrs Longlegs strides, Johnny Jones hops and Bernie Brown rolls to church in time for the service. The Reverend Hicks talks and prays, the choir sings and the people in the pews listen while Mrs Hogglehump bashes a tune on the organ. At the end they all shake hands and go home to eat their turkeys!

Choose verbs from the list to put into this passage. Use each verb once only.

hate	get
eating	grabs
enjoy	love
kisses	has
talking	opening

There's one part of Christmas

I _____ . It's not _____

my presents, because I _____

that! It's not _____ my Christmas

lunch, because I _____ my food.

It isn't even after lunch when all the adults

start _____ for ages and the

children _____ bored. No, it's

when Great Aunt Joan _____

me and _____ me under the

mistletoe. Yuk! Her chin _____

more hairs on it than my Dad's – and he's

got a beard!

⭐ **Worksheets**

Goodies and baddies

Can you think of a teacher who you hate but other children like? It's the same with the characters in the Christmas story. Each can be seen from at least two points of view.

Divide into groups and split those groups in two. Each pair of groups selects a character from the Christmas story (but don't use Mary, Joseph or Jesus). One group looks for the character's good aspects and the other group thinks of all their bad points. Use the questions on the form to help you think about the character. Compare your views with your partner group's. Make a good copy of the form and cut it out for display.

Name of character:

We selected him or her because:

What role did this character have in the Christmas story?

What clues are there to this person's character?

How could the character have acted in a different way? How could he or she have helped Mary and Joseph more?

Courtroom drama

Hold a trial for King Herod. Was he evil or did he act like a proper king? One member of the class defends him and another prosecutes. The rest of the class act as the jury.

Worksheets ✪

I was, I am, I will be good

Look closely at these sentences. Put a circle round the correct tense in the list at the side. Now write each sentence again in spaces b and c, using a different tense each time. The first one is done for you.

a I was very good and Father Christmas gave me lots of presents.

⟨past⟩
present
future

b I am very good and Father Christmas gives me lots of presents.

c I will be very good and Father Christmas will give me lots of presents.

a The wise men are handing their gifts to Mary who is smiling.

past
present
future

b ....

c ....

a I am going to make some mince pies and then I'll write my cards.

past
present
future

b ....

c ....

a Jane was singing carols and chewing a sweet at the same time!

past
present
future

b ....

c ....

Special Christmas cake

Identify the tense and then write two other versions on paper, using the other two tenses.

I am putting six spoonfuls of curry powder in the Christmas cake mixture to make it interesting. I add three litres of fizzy drink and a dog biscuit, then I mix it all together. Now I throw it into a dish and give it to my sister to eat. She isn't enjoying it very much. I wonder why!

❂ **Worksheets**

Lights, camera, action...

Here is a description of the beginning of a new Christmas film. Some verbs have been underlined. Replace them with different verbs that make it easier to imagine how the film would look. The first two are done for you.

gusted   kicking

The wind blew strongly, lifting a few leaves into the air. The clouds were dark above him and Oliver knew that soon it would rain. He had to find shelter quickly and so he walked across a field towards the well-lit farmhouse. 'It was a mistake to leave the lane,' he said to himself, but it was too late now. He came to a hedge and pulled himself through somehow, his coat catching on the branches. Oliver saw sheds on either side of him, their shapes showing against the darkening sky. He made his way past an old tractor and walked across a lawn until he was under the window. Slowly, he lifted his head and looked in.

A fire burned brightly, decorations were everywhere and a Christmas tree was in the corner. Two children were busy hanging their stockings to the side of the fireplace, their parents watching them. Everyone had smiles on their faces and the children kept looking at the parcels piled under the tree.

With a lump in his throat Oliver turned away from the window. He knew he couldn't join the family. He stopped by the gate for a last look at the stockings and decorations – and then ran to the shelter of the barns as it began to rain.

What a Christmas Eve!

Worksheets ✪

Instructions

Read the instructions for making a snowball. Now write instructions on paper for three of the activities below. Keep them concise but make sure they're really clear.

How to make a snowball

1 Cup hands and move towards each other.
2 Trap snow between hands and squeeze.
3 Move hands around lump of snow until ball shape is achieved.
4 Take aim and throw at headteacher.
5 Run around corner of playground.
6 Look innocent.

- Eating dinner
- Laying a table
- Loading a computer game
- Opening presents
- Washing up
- Pulling a cracker
- Laughing!
- Wrapping presents
- Singing carols
- Making Christmas pudding
- Decorating a tree

Group discussion

Instructions need to be

- concise
- in sequence
- clear
- complete.

Notice that the sentences in the snowball instructions have been **truncated** (this means they have been cut short).

Compare them with some of the instructions written by the class.

Discuss these points.

- Why have short sentences been used?
- Should you use complete sentences?
- Could any of the instructions be arranged in a better way?
- How could you improve the instructions?

Worksheets

© **pfp** publishing limited 2002 ISBN 1 874050 59 7 May be photocopied for use only within the purchasing institution **pfp**, 61 Gray's Inn Road, London WC1X 8TH

Shuffling sentences

Have a look at this sentence.

The children went out without coats although it was snowing heavily.

If we change the two halves of the sentence round, it still has the same meaning but sounds more dramatic.

Although it was snowing heavily, the children went out without coats.

Change these sentences around without changing the meaning and write the new version on another sheet of paper. Decide which version sounds best and why.

1 The vicar took the Christmas service, even though he felt unwell.

2 Mary thanked Tom for the present although she already had a stereo.

3 My sister threw a mince pie at me when I came home from school.

4 Father Christmas upset all his elves by whistling while he worked.

5 Prancer wanted to keep going whereas Rudolph felt he'd done enough.

6 I'm playing tricks on my brother this year because he put a rotten melon in my stocking last year.

Sometimes we can split sentences even further to make several versions of the same sentence.

The children, although it was snowing heavily, went out without coats.

Write down another variation of all the sentences. Take care not to change the meaning.

Worksheets ✪

Less is more

Read the sentence below carefully. It is far too long. Cross out all the words and phrases that can be deleted without changing the basic meaning. Write out your new sentence on paper and read it to a partner.

Comment on each other's new version.

The weather was absolutely awful, lashing with rain driven along almost horizontally by a fierce south-westerly gale as the assorted group of carol singers began to leave the centrally heated church hall and make their laborious way down the brightly lit and festive high street.

Now read these sentences. Cross out words and phrases that can be deleted without changing the basic meaning, but keep enough adjectives and adverbs to make the writing interesting.

When you've finished, compare your versions with your partner's.

1 The Three Wise Men – or Three Kings as they are often known – decided after a little discussion to call on King Herod in his great and imposing palace in Jerusalem to enquire where this new king was to be found.

2 Feeling weary and very tired, dear old Father Christmas pushed hard on his old wooden front door and gratefully entered his lonely cottage to the warming sight of a gently glowing stove and a large black pot of Christmas stew which simmered on top.

3 The brightly shining star was still hanging motionless in the night sky as the nervous and anxious shepherds began to enter the small inn where, so they had been told, the baby Jesus, the Holy Infant had been born.

4 Uncle Dan, feeling totally drained and exhausted, kicked off his shoes and sank gratefully into his favourite old armchair, determined to snatch five minutes' peace in the midst of all the frenetic Christmas activities while everyone else cleared up the kitchen!

★ **Worksheets**

All you need for **Christmas**

Underlining grammar

1 Draw lines to link these descriptions to the name of the right word class.

These words link phrases or sentences	**ADJECTIVES**
These words take the place of a noun	**NOUNS**
These are 'action' or 'doing' words	**CONJUNCTIONS /CONNECTIVES**
The name of a person, a place or a thing	**VERBS**
These words show position	**PREPOSITIONS**
These words tell us more about verbs	**PRONOUNS**
These words tell us more about nouns	**ADVERBS**

2 Spot the verbs (or verbal phrases) and nouns in the passage below. Underline verbs in green and nouns in red.

Peter was nineteen and was preparing to hang up his stocking, just as he had done for as long as he could remember. The stocking itself was old and worn with a rip in one side where Father Christmas had tried to stuff a present in a little too energetically a year or two ago. He hadn't repaired it because he thought his parents might buy him a replacement, which might be even bigger!

3 Now search for adjectives and adverbs in the next passage. Choose two different colours to underline them with.

The delicious Christmas meal was over and the family groaned contentedly at the table. In the kitchen lay the ravaged remains of the turkey, which had served them well. Cold gravy was congealing slowly in the jug and the overcooked, limp sprouts were all but cold. Once crisp roast potatoes forlornly clung to each other and the pile of dirty plates became more of a challenge every minute.

4 Working on your own or with a partner, write a passage which contains a number of pronouns and prepositions. Then swap your writing for someone else's and underline the words.

Worksheets ✪

Scriptwriting

Choose a scene from the Christmas story and turn it into a script for part of a Christmas play. Start by creating a planning sheet. Develop the sheet using these steps.

1 Characters

At the top of the sheet, list all the characters involved in the scene and be prepared to invent a few others if it helps!

2 Starting scenario

Write a sentence or two to describe where the scene takes place, what is happening when the scene begins and which characters are present.

3 Ending point

At the bottom of the sheet, describe what happens and who is present at the end of the scene.

4 Storyline

Jot down storyline headings between the two in sequential order. These mark the most important things that happen during the scene. Make it clear when characters enter or exit. Leave space under the headings to add further details.

Then you can flesh it out. Don't rush it – planning pays off!

Decide on positions – who stands where. Remember that an actor will only move on stage if you write an instruction (called a stage direction) in the script. It's like programming a computer.

Use double-spacing when writing so you can fit in anything you've forgotten.

5 Write the script

Now you can write the words for the characters to say, using the planning sheet as your guide. Really try to get into the minds of your characters. Make them speak like real people.

I decided that we had to take this advice, so my friends and I set off to follow the star.

Worksheets

Christmas news

You are a newspaper reporter in the Holy Land and you have been assigned to cover the reports of a strange, bright star and a new king. Your job is to interview up to five people to develop your story. They can be main or minor characters. From them you have to get a balanced view about these strange events.

What to do

Brainstorm lists of main and minor characters from the Christmas story and consider the events from their perspective. Divide into reporters and characters. Exchange roles on completion. Write an unbiased report based only on what you have been told. Display and compare findings.

Characters

Prepare your story well. Add a bit of personality to your character – act the part.

Reporters

Select the characters you wish to interview. Prepare appropriate questions. Make notes during interviews.

> Well, as I was coming out of my tent I couldn't help noticing that Caspar was talking very quietly to a man wearing...

> How much are you going to pay me, eh? I mean, my information's got to be worth...

> And then I heard King Herod say that he wanted all the baby boys in the area killed. Well, I mean to say...

> It is of course essential that your newspaper reports this accurately so I require my exact wording to be recorded. I know that Joseph...

Worksheets ☆

Christmas adding up

   +    = _____

   +    = _____

    +  = _____

 +  = _____

 = _____

 +  +  = _____

  +   +  = _____

 = _____

☆ **Worksheets**

Santa's sacks

Father Christmas has to put the same presents in each sack. Help him by drawing a line from each present to the right sack. One is done for you.

How many presents are in each sack? Write the number on the dotted lines.

Worksheets ✪

Find Father Christmas

Help Father Christmas find his way to the house by colouring in the right path. He mustn't get his feet wet in the streams. Then try describing where Father Christmas needs to turn.

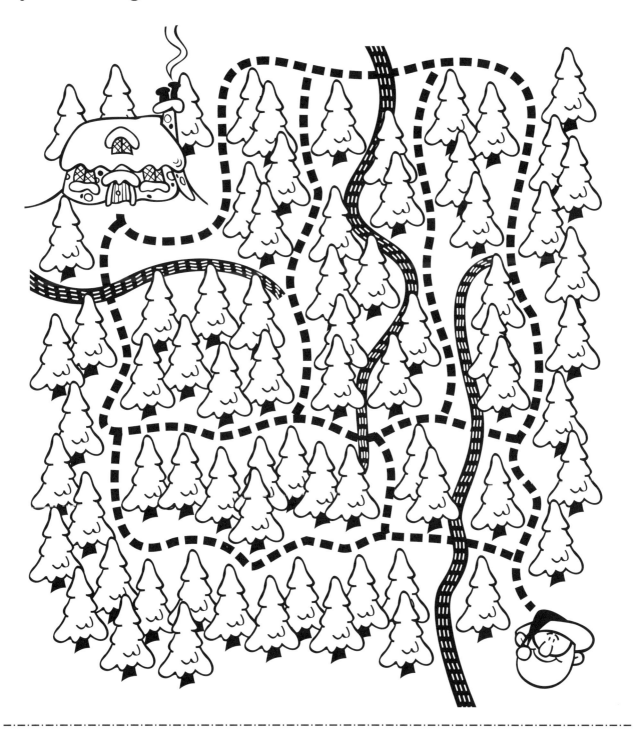

❂ Worksheets

Party biscuit problem

Here are some plates of biscuits for our Christmas party. Yum yum! But look – there are different numbers of biscuits on each plate.

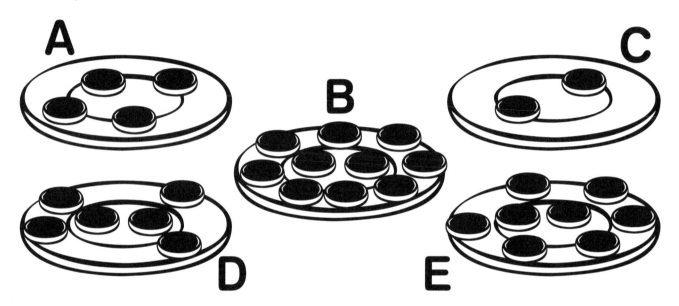

Count the biscuits on each plate and write the number in the list.

Plate A has _____ biscuits   Plate B has _____ biscuits

Plate C has _____ biscuits   Plate D has _____ biscuits

Plate E has _____ biscuits

Which plate would you like? _____

Do you think the plates are fair? _____

What could be done about it? _____

_____

134

Estimating and counting

Does Father Christmas have enough presents for everybody? Estimate how many he has then count them to check. Write your answers in the spaces.

Estimate ....

Count ....

All these carol singers will need a cup of tea. Estimate how many there are then count them to check. Write your answers in the spaces.

Estimate ....

Count ....

Estimate how many Christmas crackers there are then count them to check. Write your answers in the spaces.

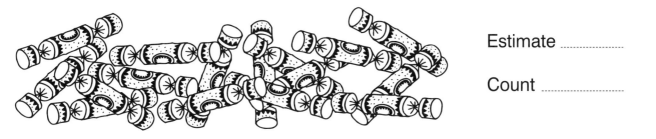

Estimate ....

Count ....

How did you get your answers? Tell the class.

● **Worksheets**

2 + 2 = Christmas!

Father Christmas wants 10 presents for each stocking. Draw lines linking two piles that add up to 10.

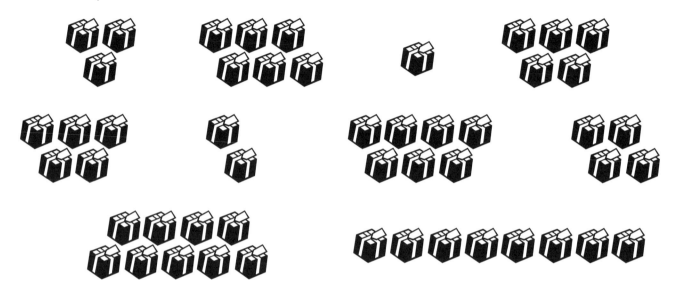

Help Father Christmas add up these presents. Write the answers in the spaces.

Now add up these numbers and write the answers in the spaces.

3 + 3 = ...   2 + 2 = ...   4 + 4 = ...   5 + 5 = ...

8 + 2 = ...   4 + 6 = ...   3 + 7 = ...   9 + 1 = ...

Worksheets ✪

Christmas card count

Children asked their teachers how many Christmas cards they received.
Here is a list of their results.

| Miss Lovely | 25 | Mr Grabbem | 3 | Mrs Fierce | 10 | Mr Hop-Off | 5 |
| Ms Mangler | 8 | Mr Twit | 1 | | | | |

Draw a pictogram here to show these results.

Now draw a block graph here to show the same results.

Which is easier to understand? _____

Why? _____

Who had the most cards? _____

Who had the smallest number of cards? _____

Whose score was in the middle (or 'average')? _____

★ **Worksheets**

All you need for Christmas

Christmas maze

Father Christmas is stuck in a maze. Help him to find a way out so he can deliver your presents.

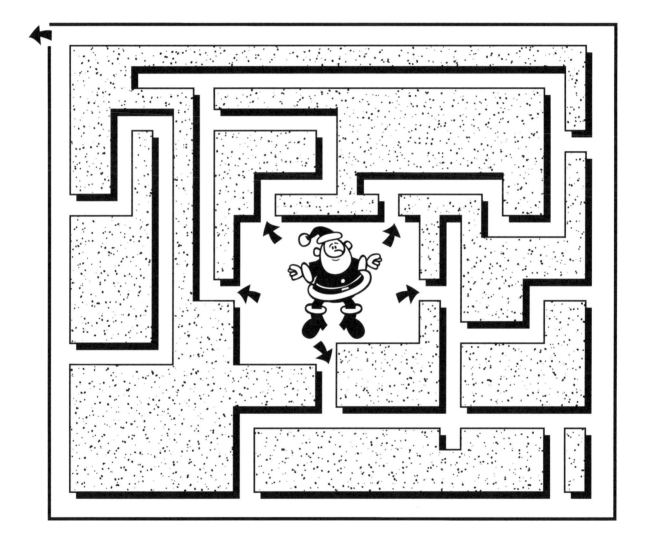

Give Father Christmas instructions to get out of the maze. Decide which exit to use and then write down your instructions using these commands.

F = go forwards, R90 = turn right 90˚, L90 = turn left 90˚

Your instructions might look like this: F\R90\F\L90… and so on.

There are lots of different routes. Try all the exits from the centre. Then work with a partner to check your results.

Worksheets ✪

138

Help Santa

Santa can't keep count of all these presents! Use times tables to work out the answers. Write the answers in the spaces.

1 There are 10 piles, each with 8 parcels. How many is that? ....

2 We have 5 sacks, each with 10 presents. That comes to…? ....

3 There are 7 shelves, each with 10 books on. How many books are there? ....

4 Here are 2 bags, each with 6 large balls. That's….? ....

5 The sleigh has got 3 pairs of reindeer to pull it. That's…? ....

Now work out the answers to these questions.
Write the answers in the spaces.

6 Here are 5 lots of 4 sweets. How many is that? ....

7 And look – 6 piles of presents, each with 5 presents. That's…? ....

8 Here are 9 sets of new handkerchiefs, each containing 5. How many? ....

Find doubles for these numbers. Write the answer in the space beside the number.

9 ....   10 ....   6 ....   5 ....

Find halves for these numbers. Write the answer in the space beside the number.

20 ....   12 ....   8 ....   16 ....   10 ....

Directions

Help Father Christmas find your house.

Father Christmas needs to find his way across town to your house. Start from the arrow on the map. On a piece of paper, write down the direction he needs to take every time he turns a corner, using the compass directions N, S, E and W. It should look something like this:

N\E\N\W\… and so on.

How many routes can you find?

Do you know the compass points in between north, south, east and west? You will need them for some routes. Write them on the compass next to the map.

Then plan a route to the other boys' and girls' houses.

Worksheets ✪

That's approximately...

The elf in charge of present wrapping has to tell Father Christmas approximately how many presents are ready. Write the answers in the spaces.

12 presents is approximately ....

18 presents is approximately ....

Check your answers with a friend and then round these numbers to the nearest 10. Remember – 5 and above go up, below 5 go down. Write your answers in the spaces.

27 balls is approximately ....   41 dolls is approximately ....

54 books is approximately ....   65 cars is approximately ....

99 CDs is approximately ....   4 walkmans is approximately ....

Round these numbers to the nearest 100. Write your answers in the spaces.

131 choc bars is approximately ....   504 videos is approximately ....

455 skateboards is approximately ....   270 mice is approximately ....

Now help the elf by estimating the number of parcels in this pile to the nearest 10. Then count the parcels and round the number to the nearest 10. Write your answers in the spaces.

Estimate ....   Count ....

All you need for Christmas

It's a wrap!

The elves have mixed up the wrapped and unwrapped presents. Find out what fraction of each pile has been wrapped. Write the answers in the spaces. The first one has been done for you.

1 ⬚⬚⬚⬚ = $\frac{1}{4}$ 2 ⬚⬚⬚⬚⬚⬚ =   3 ⬚⬚⬚ =

4 ⬚⬚⬚⬚⬚ =   5 ⬚⬚ =   6 ⬚⬚⬚⬚⬚⬚⬚⬚ =

Tell your partner the names of these fractions.

What fraction of each pile has been wrapped here?
Write the answers in the spaces.

1 ⬚⬚⬚⬚ =   2 ⬚⬚⬚⬚⬚⬚ =   3 ⬚⬚⬚ =

4 ⬚⬚⬚⬚ =   5 ⬚⬚⬚⬚⬚⬚⬚⬚⬚ =   6 ⬚⬚⬚⬚⬚⬚⬚⬚ =

Look at piles 1, 2 and 6. What do you notice?

Now, colour in $\frac{1}{2}$ of each of these piles.

1   2   3   4

And now try colouring $\frac{1}{4}$ of these shapes. Be careful – there's a trick!

5   6   7   8

Worksheets ✪

Christmas problems

Work out the answers to these questions on paper.
Remember – thinking is just as important as getting things right.

1   I've collected a load of pennies to buy new decorations. They total 3420p. How much is this in pounds and pence?

2   I have eight nephews and nieces. I have £120 to spend on them in total. How much could I spend on each?

3   On second thoughts I can only afford £100. Now how much could I spend on each?

4   Carol singers were singing in the town for 95 minutes on Monday, 1 hour on Tuesday, 80 minutes on Wednesday and 55 minutes on Thursday. How much time did they spend singing altogether?

5   I bought 30 x 19p stamps and 15 x 27p stamps for all my Christmas cards. How much did all these stamps cost?

Find different strategies and compare them with others.

How much change did I receive from £10?

6   I have five parcels to wrap, all the same size. One parcel takes 1.25m of Christmas wrapping paper. How much paper will I use in total?

How much paper will be left on a 10m roll?

8   If Father Christmas has 20 homes to visit in a village and takes $1\frac{1}{2}$ minutes in each home, how long will it be before he's finished?

9   If an elf can make 12 toys in a day, how long will it take him to make 150?

10   If another elf makes 15 toys a day, how many days will she have to work to produce 150?

Worksheets

All you need for **Christmas**

Lazy elves

1 The elves have been wasting time and have only done a fraction of their work. Put the fractions in order so that Father Christmas knows who has worked least. Start with the smallest fraction. Write your answers in the boxes.

Red Elf $\frac{3}{4}$ Green Elf $\frac{1}{2}$ Blue Elf $\frac{1}{4}$ Yellow Elf $\frac{2}{5}$ Brown Elf $\frac{1}{5}$

2 If they all had 20 parcels to wrap, how many has each elf completed? Write the answers in the boxes.

Red Elf   Green Elf   Blue Elf   Yellow Elf   Brown Elf

3 Yesterday, Blue Elf had to wrap 10 parcels in an hour. He managed 9. Show 9 out of 10 as a fraction and as a decimal fraction.

Fraction   Decimal fraction

4 The postman must deliver 25 parcels this morning. By 10am he's only delivered $\frac{1}{5}$ of them.

How many has he delivered?   What fraction is still to be delivered?

5 The Three Wise Men have 90km to travel. By the end of the fourth day they've covered 60km.

What fraction of the journey have they covered?

What fraction do they still have to cover?

Worksheets ✪

☆**Numeracy worksheet 15**

Christmas present graphs

Look at this graph of Christmas presents received by another class last year.

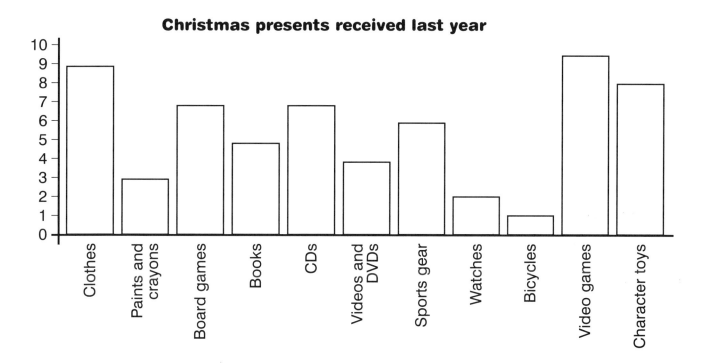

Christmas presents received last year

1 Ask your partner some questions about the graph.
   For instance

   • which type of presents were equally popular?

   • which present was least popular?

2 How would your class compare? Here's what to do.

   • Find paper and pencil.

   • Ask the class to choose their favourite present.

   • Collect data quickly without having a chat and
     draw a graph.

   • Compare your results with the graph above.

3 Now do the same to make a 'Wish-list graph' for this Christmas,
   choosing the present categories that are most popular in your class.

Worksheets

All you need for Christmas

Mental maths

There's chaos at Father Christmas's grotto! The old elves have retired and the new elves can't add or subtract large numbers. Can you help?

These numbers are the daily totals of wrapped parcels. Write the answers in the spaces.

1 348 + 252 = ...

2 146 + 98 = ...

3 807 + 299 = ...

4 509 + 311 = ...

5 1023 + 997 = ...

Think what strategies you used and ask a partner how they worked them out.

The figures below will show how many more parcels have to be wrapped. Write the answers in the spaces. Then share your strategies with a partner.

1 350 - 75 = ...

2 499 - 203 = ...

3 509 - 311 = ...

4 2300 - 1998 = ...

5 6001 - 2999 = ...

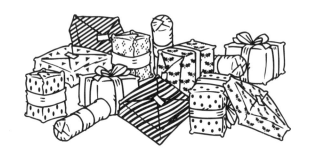

The following are the number of presents wrapped by elves each day. Write the answers in the spaces.

1 32 + 226 + 41 = ...

2 116 + 49 + 23 = ...

3 65 + 80 + 330 = ...

4 56 + 45 + 41 + 105 = ...

Now try these. Write your answers in the spaces.

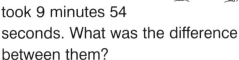

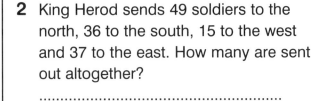

1 The first shepherd reached Jesus in 6 minutes 34 seconds. The last took 9 minutes 54 seconds. What was the difference between them?

....

2 King Herod sends 49 soldiers to the north, 36 to the south, 15 to the west and 37 to the east. How many are sent out altogether?

....

If he has 250 soldiers, how many are left at his palace?......................

3 The Three Wise Men take 10 days to reach Bethlehem. Each day the number of people they meet doubles. On the tenth day they meet 4,608 people, so how many did they meet on the first day?..............

Worksheets ✪

All you need for **Christmas**

Christmas spending

The graph shows how much parents spend on presents in different countries. Note that the vertical axis displays £ in 100s. Write answers to the questions below in the spaces.

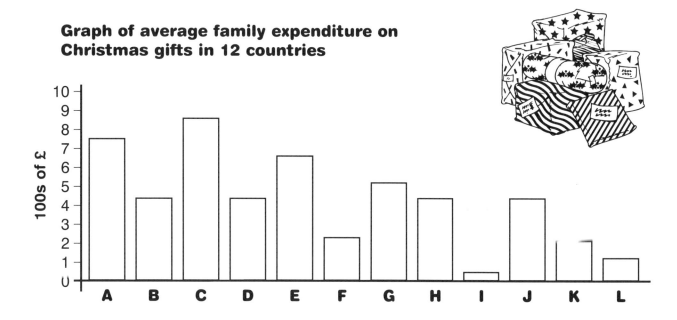

Graph of average family expenditure on Christmas gifts in 12 countries

1 How much is spent in country A?

....

2 Estimate the amounts spent in these countries.

H ....

I ....

C ....

3 Find the difference between the countries with highest and lowest expenditure.

....

4 Estimate the total expenditure for all the other countries shown on the graph. ....

5 Calculate the average expenditure.

....

6 Find the mode of the data given.

....

7 Identify which countries are below average and write possible reasons for this in the space below.

....

❂ Worksheets

All you need for **Christmas**

Maths strategies

Look carefully at the questions below. Work out how to do each in turn.
Try mental strategies before using pencil and paper or calculator.
Write your answers on paper.

1 If Father Christmas employs 36 elves, each of which can wrap 95 presents a day, how many presents should be wrapped in two days?

2 Mum sends off 44 Christmas cards. She sends 18 at 1st class post (27p) and 19 at 2nd class post (19p). How much does she pay for postage? How many did she deliver by hand?

3 If one reindeer eats 5kg of feed a day, how much would a herd of 15 eat in a week?

4 In a family of 5, Dad gave 18 presents and received 10, Mum gave 15 and received 15, Josie gave 9 and received 8, Nicci gave 10 and received 9, Joe gave 7 and received 8. Who do you think did best and why?

5 Parcelforce delivered 100,000 parcels during a 10-hour day. On average, how many parcels were delivered each hour?

6 Santa has to divide his piles of presents between 6 sacks. Which of these numbers can be exactly divided by 6?

2520   1998   330   1164

3569   1218   5978   3885   7803

Now write down the numbers that are divisible by 7, in case he finds an extra sack!

7 I buy 4 presents. The first costs £17.99, the second £23.89, the third £145.98 and the fourth £15.99. How much did I spend altogether? What was the difference between the most expensive and cheapest?

8 I buy all my Christmas gifts between 09:46 and 17:23. How long did it take me?

Worksheets ✪

Real-life maths

It's a well-known fact that everyone believes in Father Christmas so here are some 'real-life' questions, just for you! Work out the answers on paper.

1   Father Christmas has 45 presents to wrap, each requiring 95cm of wrapping paper. Should he use 2 x 20m rolls, 3 x 15m rolls or 1 x 50m?

2   If one large turkey can produce 18 normal-sized portions, how many turkeys will be required for the tennis club's annual Christmas dinner, where there will be 378 guests?

3   The elves have to fill 1,308 x 33cl bottles with 'Santa's Aromatherapy Surprise'. How many litres will they use?

4   What is the capacity of a church with 37 rows of 18-seater pews, 9 rows of 12-seater pews and 6 side pews each holding 7 people?

5   A box measures 27cm x 45cm x 16.5cm. How much ribbon will be required to decorate it? What else should you consider?

6   One carol singer walks 3.35km on one evening of carol singing. She walks 0.42km the next and 1.75km on the final evening. If her choir consists of 29 people in total and they all walked the same distances, how far did they cover between them over 3 evenings?

7   If one potato can be cut into 4 pieces before being roasted for Christmas dinner, how many potatoes will be needed to provide 190 pieces of roast potato?

8   How many jokes are there in 7 crates of 250 boxes of crackers if each box contains a dozen crackers? How many do you think are funny?

9   Parcelforce delivers 17,000 parcels in the 5 days before Christmas in Plymouth. How many parcels are delivered on average each day?

⊛ **Worksheets**

Disaster time for Santa

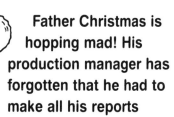

Father Christmas is hopping mad! His production manager has forgotten that he had to make all his reports concerning how many presents had been wrapped in percentages. Instead, he's done it in fractions. Useless!

Go on – sort things out, please! Write the answers in the spaces.

1 $\frac{1}{2} =$ **2** $\frac{1}{4} =$

3 $\frac{3}{4} =$ **4** $\frac{1}{3} =$

5 $\frac{1}{10} =$ **6** $\frac{2}{10} =$

7 $\frac{1}{5} =$ **8** $\frac{2}{3} =$

9 $\frac{4}{5} =$ **10** $1 =$

Now write the answers to these questions in the spaces.

1 An elf reports that a quarter of the foam bath bottles have developed leaks. What percentage is still intact? ....

2 Father Christmas discovers that mice have nibbled $\frac{3}{4}$ of the chocolate bars.

If he had 9,000 of them, how many need to be replaced? ....

3 10% of the pairs of socks on order haven't arrived. Panic! 500 were ordered, so how many are missing?
....

4 No – it gets worse! 30% are missing! How many socks are missing now? ....

5 Father Christmas has 1,800 hessian sacks for deliveries world-wide. 25% have rotted in the damp summer conditions. What percentage of the sacks is still usable? ....

How many new sacks must he make? ....

6 In one town, 750 out of a possible 1,000 children have misbehaved so frequently during the year that their chances of having a visit from Father Christmas are pretty remote.

What percentage of children have been perfect little angels? ....

7 What percentage of your class deserve a visit on Christmas Eve? ....

3-D Christmas wrapping

Father Christmas has lost the labels for the designs of the various 3-D boxes he uses to protect presents. Confusion will reign unless you help him. Unfortunately, there are a few 'dud' designs as well. Put a tick in the star by each successful design and write the name underneath the shape.

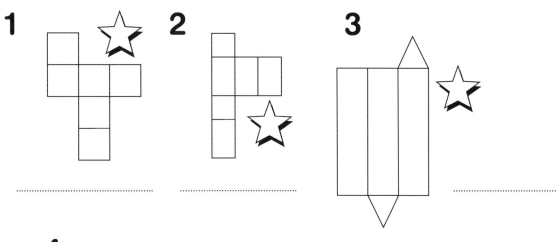

1   2   3

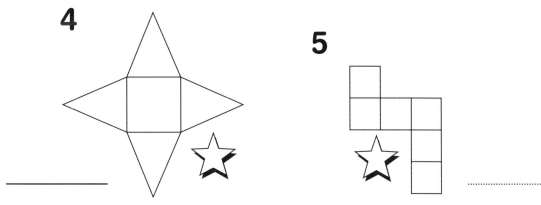

4   5

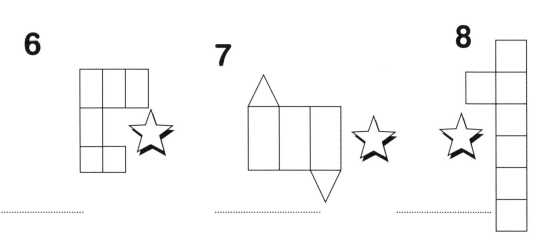

6   7   8

☆ **Worksheets**

Christmas light

Add to the Christmas lights in your home by making a table decoration or putting a red light above your stocking to help Father Christmas find it!

What you need

- switch
- wiring
- battery
- bulb
- bulb holder
- oil paint (for light bulb)

DANGER!
Electricity – only use batteries

What to do

1 Make a circuit like the one in the diagram.

2 Test it out by pressing the switch. The bulb should light up.

3 Paint the bulb red or green with oil paint.

4 Put your circuit into a table decoration or above your stocking.

5 Hide the wiring, battery and switch in a box so it looks nice.

6 Now you can use it at Christmas!

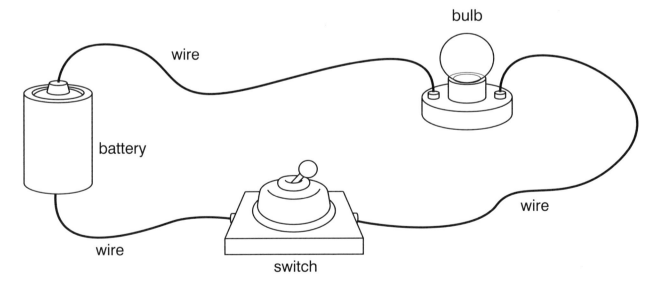

Go further: Design an electric Christmas card.

Worksheets ★

Magnetic Christmas story

Make up your own Christmas play and perform it using cardboard characters you have made yourself.

What you need

- card
- felt tips (or paint)
- scissors
- sticky tape
- 2 paperclips
- 2 magnets
- large sheet of white card

Go further

- Try different magnets.
- Try different materials for the screen.
- Find out which materials are magnetic.

What to do

1 Choose two characters and write a story for them.

2 Draw your characters on pieces of card. Make them about 12cm high. Use the line on this sheet as a guide.

3 Colour and cut out your characters.

4 Tape a paperclip to the back of each one.

5 Ask a grown up to help make a stand to hold the large sheet of card like a screen.

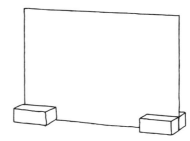

6 Colour the card with a background scene if you want one. You could have different pieces of card for different scenes.

7 Practise your play and perform it to friends by moving the magnets behind the sheet and using them to attract the paperclips on the characters in front of the sheet.

12cm – make your characters this high

★ Worksheets

All you need for Christmas

Wrapping paper ripper

Some wrapping paper is not as strong as it should be. Test some different types to find out which are best!

What you need

- **wrapping paper (as many different types as you can get)**
- **scissors**
- **2 pencils**
- **2 bulldog clips**
- **string**
- **small container**
- **hook**
- **identical weights**

What to do

1 Cut strips about 20cm long and 5cm wide from different wrapping paper. Use the lines on this sheet as a guide. Give each one a number.

2 Wrap each end of the first piece around a pencil and hold with a clip.

3 Tie string to one clip and hang the container off the other with the hook.

4 Add weights to the container carefully one at a time.

5 Note how many weights each paper can hold before tearing.

Before you start ripping up paper, make sure you predict what will happen. Does it look strong? Is it thicker than the others?

When you have finished, tell the class which of the papers were the strongest.

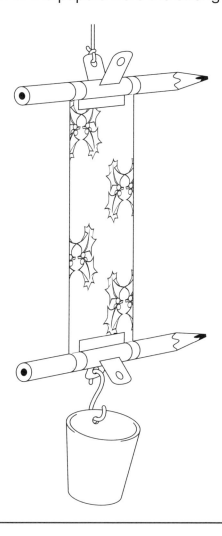

20cm

5cm

Go further
- What happens when the paper is wet?
- Try to find out if the more money you spend, the better the paper!

Worksheets ✪

Animals at Christmas

There are animals in the Christmas story. The donkey carried Mary and the Three Wise Men rode on camels. Can you think of any others? What did those animals need on their journeys? Tell the class.

Think about any pets you have at home. What do these pets need? Write it down here.

My pet is a

My pet needs

Think of something nice that will happen to your pet over Christmas. Write it down here.

Tell your class how you will care for your pets over Christmas. Remember – animals won't understand all that's going on!

Put ticks in the table to show what your pet likes and dislikes.

	My pet likes it	My pet dislikes it
Human food		
Normal pet food and water		
Chocolate		
Sweets and fizzy drinks		
Crackers going bang		
Lots of noise and excitement		
Being taken out/stroked/ cared for		
Being ignored/ shut in/forgotten		

✪ **Worksheets**

Wet Christmas

Father Christmas got soaking wet last year. He has asked if anyone can invent a waterproof Father Christmas outfit in time for this Christmas Eve.

What you need

- samples of different materials from your teacher
- small bowl of water
- pipette
- towel

My waterproof outfit

What to do

1 Find out which of these materials soak up water and which are waterproof. Drip water on with the pipette and record your results in the chart below.

2 Decide which materials can be made into clothes. Select the best, and design a waterproof outfit. Draw your outfit in the space provided. Use arrows to show what the clothes are made of. Colour it in.

Is it waterproof?

Material	✔	✗
Plastic		
Cotton		
Wood		
Rubber		
Stone		

Worksheets ✪

We love Christmas food!

What you need

- **lots of different foods, snacks and drinks (but just use pictures of things that go off quickly, like meat and milk)**

- **pencil and paper**

Just think – soon we will be eating… turkey… roast potatoes… stuffing… Brussels sprouts… cakes… puddings… sweets… chocolates… yum – lovely!

Write down the Christmas foods you like best.

Some foods are good for us and some are not so good. How healthy are your favourites? Let's find out more!

What to do

1 Write these headings on three pieces of paper and lay them out on the table.

   Good for us

   Too much is harmful

   Don't know

2 Sort your samples of foods, snacks and drinks into piles beside each of the labels.

3 Make a chart of your results like the one below.

4 Compare your decisions with other groups. Answer the questions 'Why is this food good for me?' 'Why is this food harmful?'

5 Add these foods and drinks to your chart if you haven't got them already.

   - salt
   - potatoes
   - burgers
   - fizzy drinks
   - sausages
   - cream
   - alcohol
   - biscuits

   - cabbage
   - tea
   - chips
   - bacon
   - butter
   - toffee
   - water
   - chocolate

Good for us	Too much is harmful	Don't know

Worksheets

Fragile – handle with care!

Find suitable materials for protecting and transporting fragile Christmas presents.

What you need

- fragile objects such as biscuits
- selection of packaging materials and structures
- sticky tape to seal packages

What to do

Whole class

Agree on choice of fragile objects. Design a test for the packaging, such as throwing, dropping or hitting it. Discuss how to make the test fair.

Alone or in pairs

1 Design package and identify materials to be used. Justify your decisions.

2 Create and test your packaging, applying the 'fair test' rules.

3 Record results, draw conclusions and redesign if required.

Compare your results and learn from the experience of other groups. As a class reach conclusions concerning materials and packaging design and produce recommendations.

Go further
- Compare your designs and materials with those used in shops and industry.

Worksheets ✪

Teeth

Colour in the four different sorts of teeth in your mouth.

Colour incisors yellow.

Colour canines orange.

Colour premolars red.

Colour molars green.

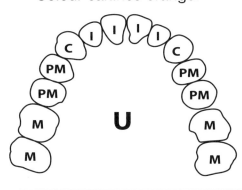

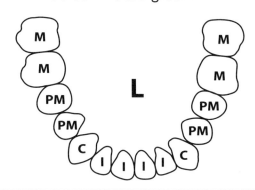

What do different teeth do? Draw lines to link the type of tooth to the best description.

Grind and chew	**INCISORS**
Grip	**CANINES**
Grind and chew	**PREMOLARS**
Cut	**MOLARS**

How often should we brush our teeth?

....

When should we clean our teeth?

....

Define these words and name two examples of each.

Herbivore ....

....

Carnivore ....

....

Omnivore ....

....

Go further
- Find out what sort of teeth occur in other animals and make conclusions about their diets. Look at dogs, cats, rats, mice, cows, goats – and lions and elephants.

⭐ **Worksheets**

Candle experiment

When a candle burns, it uses oxygen from the air. This experiment shows how vital that oxygen is!

What you need

- **saucer/dish**
- **candle**
- **matches**
- **jam jar**
- **water**
- **stopwatch**

WARNING!
Fire is dangerous – take care!

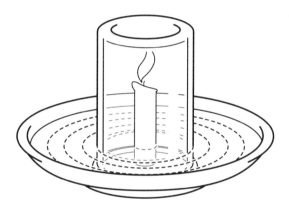

What to do

1 Fix candle firmly to saucer.

2 Fill saucer with water and light candle. Take care.

3 Start the stopwatch and slowly lower upside-down jam jar over the candle until it rests on the saucer.

4 Observe and record changes to the flame. Note how long the candle burns.

5 Try changing these things and note the results.

- Size/shape of jam jar.

- Size of candle.

- Speed of jam jar's descent.

- Quantity of water in saucer.

Questions

1 What effect does the water have?

2 What happens to the flame after the jam jar is lowered?

3 What is the relationship between size of jam jar and time?

4 How did you ensure a 'fair test'?

Go further
- Find out what air is made of.
- Find out how to put out a fire.

Worksheets ✪

Christmas waste

What you need

- lots of different cartons, wrappers, labels, bottles and other packaging

Whenever we buy anything, there always seems to be a lot that we have to throw away. One of the big problems these days is how to get rid of waste.

You hope to get a few presents for Christmas, but have you ever thought about how much is thrown away afterwards?

What to do

1 Organise the materials into groups of different source materials, such as glass, paper, foil and so on. You'll have to have some mixed categories.

2 Decide which can be returned to their original state, which can be composted and which can be recycled.

3 Discuss the questions with the class.

Questions

1 What about the rest? What happens to those materials?

2 What are the purposes of packaging?

3 How much packaging is necessary for keeping the contents safe or in good condition? How much is just for show?

4 Which of the materials to be thrown away are non-replaceable Earth's resources?

Suggested activity

Everyone in the class collects non-food rubbish left over from Christmas in bin-liners. Bring them into school on a day after the Christmas holiday and sort, classify and weigh the total.

Using ICT, record and present these findings and make recommendations to other groups – classes, parents, or the local council and MP.

Go further
- Find out what problems waste disposal causes.

⊛ **Worksheets**

All you need for Christmas

Christmas mix

What you need

- plastic bowls
- hot and cold water
- magnet
- small quantities of paper, plastic, metal, chocolate, salt, sugar, rock, sand, coffee, butter
- glitter

Different materials sometimes become mixed together. This can happen in the real world where, for example, metals can be found in rock. It also occurs as part of the manufacturing process where several materials are used to produce the end product. It can also happen by mistake!

Some materials, once mixed, cannot be separated, but some can. To be able to predict the behaviour of materials in mixes, you need to know some of the properties of materials.

What to do

1 Draw a table like the one below and try some different materials.

2 Mix up some sugar and sand. Find a way to separate them and write instructions in up to four short sentences.

3 Mix together salt, sand and iron filings. Find a way to separate them and write instructions.

4 It's Christmas so test the properties of glitter. Then mix some with salt and sand and find a process for separating them. Write instructions.

Material	Does it dissolve in cold water?	Does it melt in hot water?	Is it magnetic?	Does it float?

Worksheets ★

I am what I eat!

We all need to eat a balanced diet. How will your Christmas eating measure up?

There are lots of lovely things to eat, especially at Christmas, but we need to make sure we eat a balanced diet – the right amounts of everything.

Food gives us five main types of goodness. Each is broken down by enzymes which are found in the body. Without enzymes, we would be unable to get any goodness from our food!

The five groups of goodness are

- proteins
- carbohydrates
- fats
- vitamins
- minerals.

What to do

Find examples of Christmas foods they are in, where they are stored in the body and what their purpose is. Then fill in the table below.

Go further

- Keep a record of all the things you eat on Christmas Day. Write them down and note the type of goodness. Make a table of the results.

	Found in (foods)	Stored in (organ of the body)	Used for (purpose)
PROTEIN			
CARBOHYDRATES			
FATS			
VITAMINS			
MINERALS			

❂ **Worksheets**

Where does it all go? 1

What you need

- scissors
- sheet of paper
- sticky tape or glue

Just think of all the different food you're going to eat over Christmas. You know it all goes into your stomach, but do you know all the other bits and pieces inside you? Let's find out!

Here are the names of the major organs of the digestive system and on the next page there are pictures of them. All you have to do is pair them up. Be careful, because someone has put in a few other words which have nothing to do with eating!

What to do

1 Cut out the drawings of parts of the body on the next sheet.

2 Stick them in the right order and position on a plain piece of paper.

3 Cut out the correct names of parts from the words below and use them to label the body system you have created.

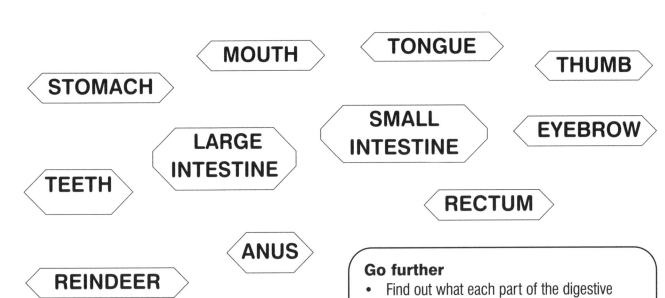

MOUTH   TONGUE   THUMB

STOMACH

LARGE INTESTINE   SMALL INTESTINE   EYEBROW

TEETH

RECTUM

ANUS

REINDEER

OESOPHAGUS

Go further
- Find out what each part of the digestive system does with your food and drink.
- Find out what other organs serve the digestive system and how.

Worksheets ✪

Where does it all go? 2

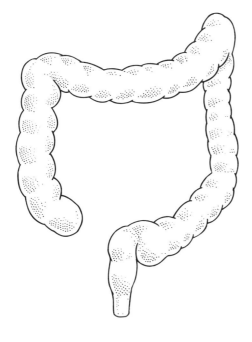
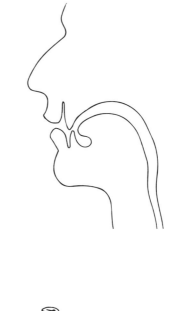

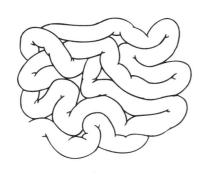
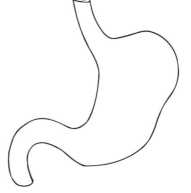

pfp © **pfp** publishing limited 2002 ISBN 1 874050 59 7 May be photocopied for use
only within the purchasing institution **pfp**, 61 Gray's Inn Road, London WC1X 8TH

★ **Worksheets**

Christmas lights 1

Make your own Christmas lights using different sorts of circuits and switches.

What you need

- **switch or switch-making materials**
- **wiring**
- **battery**
- **3 or more bulbs**
- **bulb holders for bulbs**

DANGER!
Electricity – only use batteries

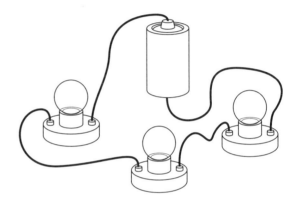

What to do

1 Construct a series circuit like the one in the picture. Make a version with one bulb, then with two and finally with three.

What do you notice about the glow from each bulb – and what does this tell you?

Why does this happen?

Where is this type of circuit used at Christmas?

2 Predict what will happen if you take out one of the bulbs. Then test.

Prediction

Test

3 Draw a circuit diagram on paper for some Christmas lights at home. You could add lights to table top decorations, the top of the tree or even up the stairs to guide Father Christmas!

4 Build and test the circuit. Hide the battery, switches and wires when you put the lights on display.

Worksheets ✪

Christmas lights 2

1 What is this type of circuit called?

2 If this circuit was used for Christmas tree lights, what would happen if one bulb was broken or missing?

3 Draw a circuit diagram of the layout shown on paper and then construct and test it.

4 There is no switch in this circuit. Put one in. Test whether the position of the switch affects the lighting.

DANGER!
Electricity – only use batteries

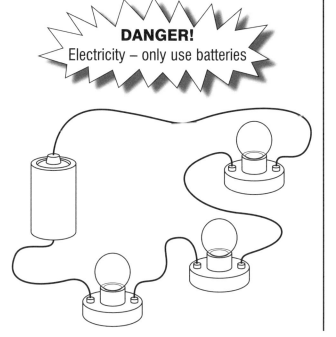

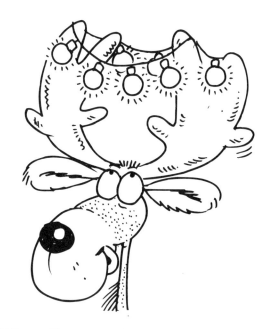

What effect do different positions of the switch have on the circuit?

Go further
- Try more than one switch and vary the positions. Remember – always predict the outcome before you test
- Develop your own types of switches. Include additional resources in the circuit, such as buzzers, bells and flashing lights.

★ **Worksheets**

Norway

Find out about Norway and the Norwegian Christmas and fill in the factfinder.

Colour in the flag

Norwegian Christmas

The Christmas meal traditionally starts with a rice pudding containing a lucky almond. A bowl is given to the barn elf to make sure he watches the livestock and doesn't get up to his usual tricks. Pork is the main course.

Norwegians used to have a yule log which was so huge it stuck out into the room. As it burned it was pushed further into the

fireplace. These days the Christmas tree is taking over as the main source of light and decoration.

Factfinder

Capital .... Language ....

Frontiers with ....

Seas/Oceans ....

Industries ....

Highest Mt.. Main river(s) ....

Main religion .... Population ....

Find three additional facts

1 ....

2 ....

3 ....

Worksheets ✪

Norway

The ancient Norse figure *Julesvenn* comes on Christmas Eve with gifts for good children.

After Christmas the children have a custom called *Julebukk* – trick or treating!

Pepperkaker (Norwegian ginger bread)

- 100g butter

- 200g sugar

- 200g corn syrup or golden syrup

- 2 tsp ground cinnamon

- 2 tsp ground cloves

- 2 tsp ground ginger

- 600g flour

- 2 eggs

- Preheat the oven to 180˚C (Gas mark 4)

1 Melt, mix and cool the butter, sugar and syrup.

2 Mix in the eggs and spices. Then mix in the flour to form a hard dough. Leave to cool for 24 hours.

3 Sprinkle flour on a board or table to prevent the dough from sticking and roll out the dough to a thin (2mm) wafer. Cut it into Christmas shapes.

4 Place the shapes on a greased baking sheet. Make sure all the shapes on a single sheet are of equal thickness. Put them in the oven for 5–7 minutes. They should have a healthy tanned look when ready. *'God Jul!'*

Go further with ICT
Access the Internet to find out
- more about *Julesvenn*
- how birds are helped before the Christmas meal
- the full Christmas menu in Norway.

❂ **Worksheets**

Greece

Find out about Greece and the Greek Christmas and fill in the factfinder.

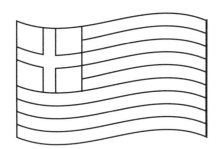

Colour in the flag

Greek Christmas

Christmas is less important than Easter in the Eastern Orthodox Church. On Christmas Eve children go from house to house singing *kalanda* (carols) and offering good wishes. There is a great feast at Christmas with pork and *christopsomo* (Christ's bread) – special large loaves

decorated to show the family trade or profession. Basil is the most common

Factfinder

Capital .... Language ....

Frontiers with ....

Seas/Oceans ....

Industries ....

Highest Mt... Main river(s) ....

Main religion... Population ....

Find three additional facts

1 ....

2 ....

3 ....

Worksheets ✪

Greece

Christmas plant. It is traditionally dipped in holy water and sprinkled around the house to keep the *Killantzaroi* away from the house.

Gifts are exchanged on St Basil's Day (1 January).

 ## Kourambiethes (shortbread)

This is a traditional Greek biscuit. Greek families make them at Christmas as the cloves are a reminder of the spices that the Wise Men brought to Jesus. As they cook you will notice the room fill with their sweet smell. These ingredients make about 25 biscuits.

- 225g softened unsalted butter

- 2 egg yolks

- 50g caster sugar

- 100g chopped almonds

- 270g plain flour

- 25 cloves

- 450g icing-sugar

- Preheat the oven to 180°C (Gas mark 4).

1 Mix the butter and the sugar together with a fork until it becomes creamy and a pale yellow colour.

2 Mix in the egg yolks (you might need an adult to help you separate the egg yolks from the egg white). Then stir in the flour and the almonds and mix everything together until you get a smooth dough.

3 Roll out a strip of the dough about 3cm wide. Cut this into 20 pieces. Put a clove on the top of each slice.

4 Put the slices on a greased baking sheet. Leave a little bit of room between the slices, because they grow bigger when they are cooking. Put them in the oven and bake them for 20–25 minutes.

5 When the shortbread is cooked, take it out of the oven and cover the top of each piece with icing sugar.

Go further with ICT

Access the Internet to find out
- what the *Killantzaroi* are
- what 'the renewal of waters' is on 1 January
- the extent to which Christmas trees are used
- if Greeks decorate their homes at Christmas.

✪ **Worksheets**

All you need for **Christmas**

Poland

Find out about Poland and the Polish Christmas and fill in the factfinder.

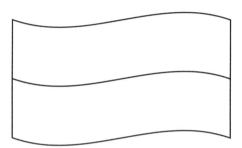

Colour in the flag

Polish Christmas

Christmas starts with presents on St Nicholas' Day (6 December) when the saint visits everyone. On Christmas Day the Star Man visits everyone – also with presents. The Star of Bethlehem is the most common image. It marks the end of fasting and the beginning of feasting. Christmas is known as *Bozz Narodzenie* but is usually referred to as

---

Factfinder

Capital .... **Language** ....

Frontiers with ....

Seas/Oceans ....

Industries ....

Highest Mt... **Main river(s)** ....

Main religion .... **Population** ....

Find three additional facts

1 ....

2 ....

3 ....

Worksheets ✪

Poland

Gwiazdka – which means Little Star. The Christmas feast has twelve courses – one for each apostle. It is traditional to have a spare seat at the table in case a stranger arrives.

Mazurek (Christmas fruit bars)

A long time ago in cold countries like Poland and Britain it was very difficult to find fresh food in the winter. This is why many traditional Christmas foods, such as mince pies, Christmas pudding and these Polish biscuits are made from dried ingredients, which can be stored and kept for a long time. This recipe will make about 40 small biscuits.

- 350g sugar
- 225g plain flour
- 100g butter
- 3 eggs
- 45ml (3tbs) double cream
- 200g sultanas
- 225g pitted dates
- 175g chopped nuts
- juice of 1 orange
- juice of 1 lemon
- 450g dried fruit (mixed)

- Preheat the oven to 180°C (Gas mark 4)

1 Mix two-thirds of the sugar with the flour. Then mix them both with the butter to make a creamy paste.

2 Beat one egg, then add both the egg and the cream to the flour, sugar and butter mixture.

3 Spread the mixture evenly in a greased tin (about 38 x 25cm). Put it in the oven for about 20 minutes.

4 While it is baking, mix the remaining two eggs with the sugar, lemon juice and dried fruit and nuts.

5 When the pastry mixture has cooked take it out of the oven. Pour the fruity mixture into the tin and spread it evenly over the pastry base. Then put it back in the oven and bake it for another 20 minutes.

6 Leave the mixture to cool and then cut it into bars.

Go further with ICT
Access the Internet to find out
- the traditional Polish Christmas meal
- more about the Star Man
- the meaning of *Pasterka*
- if Poles decorate their homes at Christmas.

Worksheets

Ireland

Find out about Ireland and the Irish Christmas and fill in the factfinder.

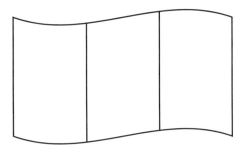

Colour in the flag

Irish Christmas

Christmas is a time for religious celebration more than parties. The Christmas tree is not widely used. Most families have cribs and candles, decorated with greenery, are placed in windows on Christmas Eve to help light the way for the Holy Family or any other travellers. Bread and milk are left

out for Mary, Joseph and the baby Jesus. Father Christmas is becoming more popular in some families.

Factfinder

Capital .... Language ....

Frontiers with ....

Seas/Oceans ....

Industries ....

Highest Mt.. Main river(s) ....

Main religion .... Population ....

Find three additional facts

1 ....

2 ....

3 ....

Worksheets ✪

© **pfp** publishing limited 2002 ISBN 1 874050 59 7 May be photocopied for use only within the purchasing institution **pfp**, 61 Gray's Inn Road, London WC1X 8TH

Ireland

Irish spice bread

This variation on Irish soda bread will keep moist for several days, and actually improves somewhat during this period. This recipe makes enough for about eight portions.

- 275g plain flour

- 2 tsp baking powder

- $\frac{1}{2}$ tsp baking soda

- 1 tsp mixed spice (cinnamon, nutmeg and allspice)

- $\frac{1}{2}$ tsp ground ginger

- 110g light brown sugar

- 50g chopped candied peel

- 175g raisins, plain or golden

- 110g butter

- 175g golden syrup

- 1 large egg, beaten

- 60ml (4tbs) milk

- Preheat the oven to 170°C (Gas mark 3)

1 Sift the flour into a mixing bowl with the soda and baking powder, and the mixed spice and ginger.

2 Add the brown sugar, chopped peel and raisins. Mix it all together. and then make a well in the centre.

3 Gently melt the butter with the syrup together over a low heat, then pour them into the well in the mixture.

4 Add the beaten egg and milk and mix very well. Pour the mixture into a greased 1kg bread tin.

5 Put the tin in the oven and bake for 40–50 minutes.

Go further with ICT
Access the Internet to find out
- the traditional Irish Christmas meal
- if the Irish decorate their homes at Christmas
- what happens on St Stephen's Day
- if and when presents are exchanged.

Worksheets

All you need for Christmas

The Netherlands

Find out about the Netherlands and the Dutch Christmas and fill in the factfinder.

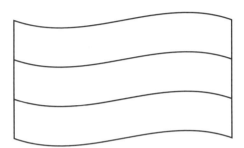

Colour in the flag

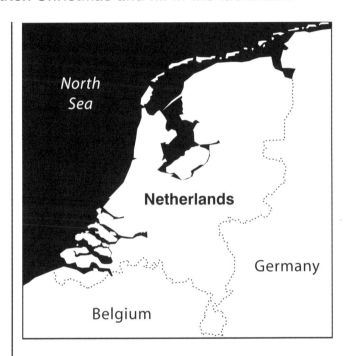

Dutch Christmas

Father Christmas is called *Sinterklaas* in the Netherlands. He arrives in Amsterdam by ship and everything closes down as people watch him arrive, accompanied by his servant. There is a great parade which ends at the palace where the royal children have to give an account of their behaviour over the last year – just as all Dutch

Factfinder

Capital .... Language ....

Frontiers with ....

Seas/Oceans ....

Industries ....

Highest Mt.. Main river(s)....................................

Main religion... Population ....

Find three additional facts

1 ....

2 ....

3 ....

Worksheets ✪

The Netherlands

children have to do. Presents are exchanged on St Nicholas' Eve (5 December). They are called 'surprises', because they are disguised as much as possible. Each is accompanied by a short poem.

Nobody gives presents on Christmas Day. 26 December is also a holiday and is called 'Second Christmas Day'.

Banketletter (pastry initials)

In the Netherlands, each person has one of these pastries made in the shape of the first letter of their name. They are put around the table to show the people where to sit for their Christmas dinner. These ingredients make about 10 large pastries.

- 400g frozen puff pastry (defrosted)

- 200g ground almonds

- 200g caster sugar

- grated rind and juice of one lemon

- 1 beaten egg

- water

- Preheat the oven to 190°C (Gas mark 5)

1 Mix the almonds with the lemon juice and sugar. Knead the mixture until you get a thick paste.

2 With your hands, roll pieces of the almond paste into thin sausage shapes about 25cm long. Wrap the sausages in greaseproof paper and leave them in the fridge for 30 minutes. (You can roll out your pastry while it is cooling.)

3 Roll out the puff pastry into strips (about 8cm wide, 25cm long and ½cm thick). Put an almond paste sausage along the middle of each piece of pastry. Rub a little bit of water along the long edges of the pastry (this helps to stop it coming undone). Fold the pastry over the almond sausage and stick the edges together, You should now have a long sausage roll.

4 Shape the rolls into whatever letters you want. Beat the egg with a fork and brush a little on to each shape. Bake them on a greased baking tray for 25–30 minutes.

Go further with ICT
Access the Internet to find out
- the traditional Dutch Christmas meal
- if Christmas trees are popular in Dutch homes
- how the Dutch conceal their 'surprises' and why.

✪ **Worksheets**

All you need for Christmas

France

Find out about France and the French Christmas and fill in the factfinder.

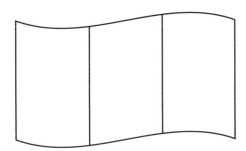

Colour in the flag

French Christmas

Father Christmas is called *Père Noël* in France. He is accompanied by *Père Fouettard* – a strict person who reminds *Père Noël* how each child has behaved during the year! Present-giving customs vary across France. Some lucky children have a visit on St Nicholas' Eve (5 December) – and again at Christmas. In other places *le petit Jesus* delivers the

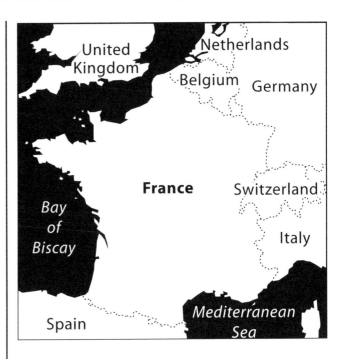

Christmas gifts. Adults normally have to wait until New Year's Day to exchange gifts.

Factfinder

Capital .... Language ....

Frontiers with ....

Seas/Oceans ....

Industries ....

Highest Mt .... Main river(s) ....

Main religion .... Population ....

Find three additional facts

1 ....

2 ....

3 ....

Worksheets ✪

France

Langues de chat (cats' tongues)

A crunchy, buttery biscuit which can be served on its own or with ice cream or sorbets.

- 60g butter, softened

- 75ml icing sugar

- 1 large egg

- 1 egg yolk

- a few drops vanilla essence

- 150ml flour

- Preheat the oven to 190°C (Gas mark 5).

1 Lightly spread softened butter onto a baking sheet.

2 Place the rest of the butter in a bowl, add the sugar and beat. Add the egg, egg yolk and vanilla and beat again. Add the flour while stirring the mixture and stir well until it is smooth.

3 Place the batter into a pastry bag with a plain tip about 7.5mm wide. Squeeze out strips of the batter onto the baking tray in 6–8 cm lengths. Keep them slightly separated so they don't stick together while baking.

4 Place them in the oven for 8–10 minutes, until golden brown at the edges and lightly browned on top. Cool the biscuits on the baking trays. Remove them with a spatula when cooled.

5 Dust the biscuits with icing sugar and/or dip them halfway into melted chocolate.

Go further with ICT

Access the Internet to find out

- the meaning of *réveillon*
- the importance of the Nativity crib in France
- if Christmas trees are popular in France.

Worksheets

All you need for Christmas

Denmark

Find out about Denmark and the Danish Christmas and fill in the factfinder.

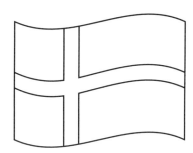

Colour in the flag

Danish Christmas

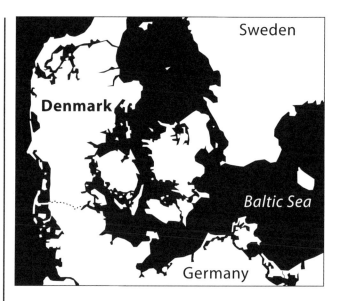

The main meal in Denmark *starts* at midnight on Christmas Eve. Talk about staying up late! The dessert is a special rice pudding which contains a single lucky almond. If you find it you'll have good luck all year!

Father Christmas is called *Julemanden* and is very similar to Father Christmas in Britain. He

delivers presents in a sack and he has a sleigh pulled by reindeer. He is assisted by elves called *Juul Nisse*, who are said to live in attics. They eat the milk and rice pudding left out by kind children.

Factfinder

Capital .... Language ....

Frontiers with ....

Seas/Oceans ....

Industries ....

Highest Mt .... Main river(s) ....

Main religion .... Population ....

Find three additional facts

1 ....

2 ....

3 ....

Worksheets ✪

pfp

Denmark

Pebernødder (pepper nuts)

Children in Denmark make these biscuits as Christmas tree treats. When they are cooked they can be wrapped in bright-coloured paper or material and hung on the tree. This recipe makes about 30 biscuits.

- 100g butter or margarine

- 100g sugar

- 1 beaten egg

- 250g flour

- 5ml (1tsp) sodium bicarbonate

- 5ml (1tsp) powdered ginger

- 5ml (1tsp) ground cardamom

- Preheat the oven to 180°C (Gas mark 4).

1 Mix the sugar and butter together with a fork until they are smooth and creamy and a pale yellow colour. Beat the egg and then mix it in with the butter and sugar paste.

2 Mix together all the dried ingredients (except the sodium bicarbonate) in a separate dish.

3 Mix the sodium bicarbonate with a little bit of cold water. Add it to the bowl of dried ingredients.

4 Mix the butter/sugar paste and the dried ingredients together really well and then knead the whole mixture until it is a smooth dough.

5 If you can, leave the dough for one hour so that it can settle down from all the pummelling you have given it. Then, roll it out into a thin sausage shape, and cut it into 3cm long pieces.

6 Bake the biscuits on a well greased baking sheet for about 20 minutes until they are brown.

Go further with ICT
Access the Internet to find out if the Danes
- have a Christmas tree and decorate it
- enjoy a main course of turkey
- exchange presents on Christmas Day.

Worksheets

All you need for Christmas

Germany

Find out about Germany, the German Christmas and fill in the factfinder.

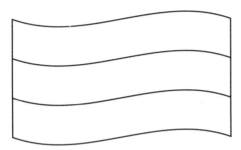

Colour in the flag

German Christmas

Christmas celebrations begin on the fourth Sunday before Christmas with the lighting of the first candle on the Advent wreath. On St Nicholas' Day (6 December), *St Nickolaus* brings the children presents if they've been good!

The Christmas tree tradition started in Germany. The *Bescherung* (giving of gifts)

Factfinder

Capital .... Language ....

Frontiers with ....

Seas/Oceans ....

Industries ....

Highest Mt.. Main river(s) ....

Main religion .... Population ....

Find three additional facts

1 ....

2 ....

3 ....

Worksheets ✪

Germany

takes place on Christmas Eve and afterwards carols are sung around the tree. Many people then attend church.

There is another holiday on 6 January to mark the visit of the Three Kings.

Schwarz-weissgebäck (black and white biscuits)

These are traditional German Christmas biscuits. The chocolate and vanilla swirls make them a very pretty treat. These ingredients will make about 30 biscuits.

- 300g plain flour
- 200g butter
- 100g caster sugar
- a few drops vanilla essence
- 1 beaten egg
- 1 egg yolk
- 10ml (2tsp) cocoa
- Preheat the oven to 180°C (Gas mark 4).

1 Sift the flour. Mix the butter and the flour together until the mixture is quite smooth. Then add the vanilla essence and the caster sugar and mix them all together well.

2 Whisk together the egg and the extra egg yolk (you might want an adult to help you separate the egg yolk from the egg white). Put the eggy mix in with the flour, butter and sugar paste and mix everything together into a dough.

3 Take the dough out of the bowl and make it into two balls.

4 Put one ball to one side and mix the cocoa into the other – you will have to knead it very well to mix the cocoa in. Put both balls in the fridge for about 30 minutes.

5 With a rolling pin roll out both balls until they are flat – about 1cm thick. Lay the dark pastry sheet on top of the light pastry sheet and gently roll them up (so it looks like a swiss-roll).

6 Carefully cut the roll into 2cm slices. Put the slices on a well greased baking tray and bake them in the oven for 15 minutes.

Go further with ICT
Access the Internet to find out
- the meaning of *Christkind*
- the meaning of *Weihnachtsgans* and what accompanies it
- if German families have Christmas crackers
- what *Knecht Rupprecht*, *Pelznickle* and *Ru-Klas* have in common.

✪ **Worksheets**

All you need for Christmas

Artwork display ideas

Teacher resources ⭐

Suggested symbols and sketches to be replaced by children's ideas

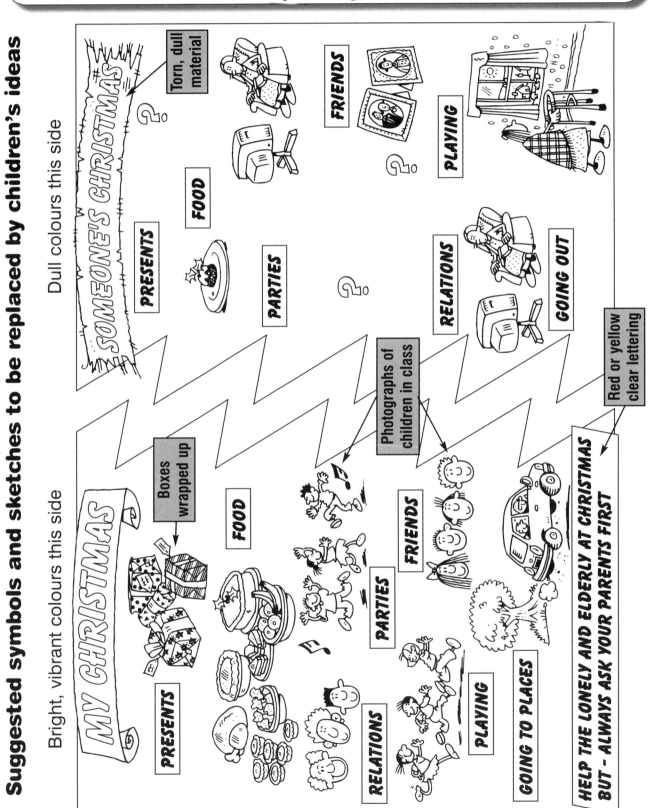

Dull colours this side

Torn, dull material

SOMEONE'S CHRISTMAS

PRESENTS

FOOD

PARTIES

FRIENDS

PLAYING

RELATIONS

GOING OUT

Bright, vibrant colours this side

Boxes wrapped up

Photographs of children in class

Red or yellow clear lettering

MY CHRISTMAS

PRESENTS

FOOD

PARTIES

FRIENDS

RELATIONS

PLAYING

GOING TO PLACES

HELP THE LONELY AND ELDERLY AT CHRISTMAS BUT - ALWAYS ASK YOUR PARENTS FIRST

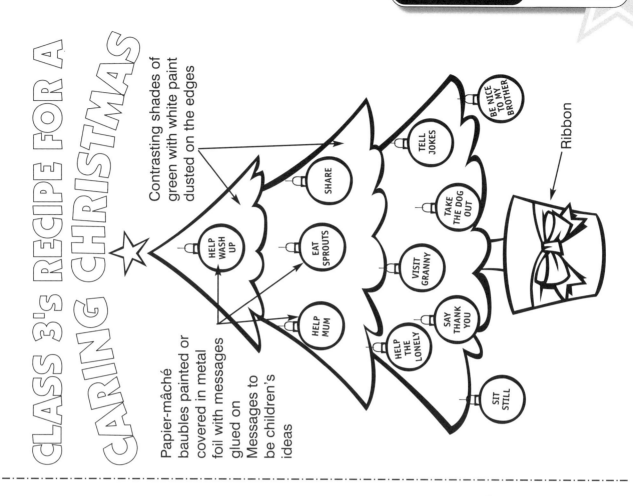

CLASS 3's RECIPE FOR A CARING CHRISTMAS

Contrasting shades of green with white paint dusted on the edges

Papier-mâché baubles painted or covered in metal foil with messages glued on
Messages to be children's ideas

Ribbon

HELP WASH UP
SHARE
EAT SPROUTS
TELL JOKES
BE NICE TO MY BROTHER
TAKE THE DOG OUT
VISIT GRANNY
HELP MUM
HELP THE LONELY
SAY THANK YOU
SIT STILL

Background detail painted

Straw on cardboard to give 3-D effect

SHARE THE WONDER OF THE BIRTH

Main figures padded with newspaper or material to create 3-D effect

Self-portraits in costume – costumes could be cloth with decoration printed on the kings' outfits

Real straw

❂ **Teacher resources**

All you need for Christmas

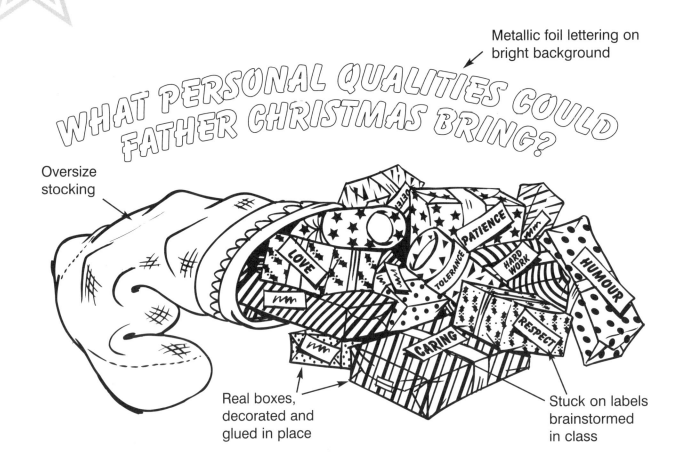

WHAT PERSONAL QUALITIES COULD FATHER CHRISTMAS BRING?

Metallic foil lettering on bright background

Oversize stocking

Real boxes, decorated and glued in place

Stuck on labels brainstormed in class

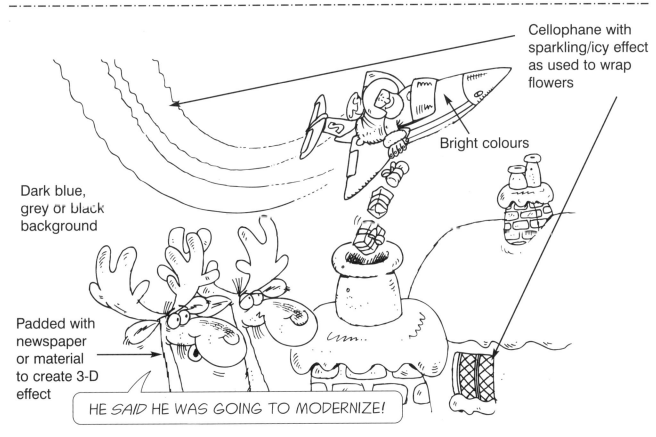

Cellophane with sparkling/icy effect as used to wrap flowers

Bright colours

Dark blue, grey or black background

Padded with newspaper or material to create 3-D effect

HE *SAID* HE WAS GOING TO MODERNIZE!

Teacher resources ✪

Table decorations

What you need

- card
- scissors
- paint, felt tips, glitter, cotton wool, etc.
- sticky tape or stapler

diagram

diagram

1 Choose a shape and enlarge it to the size you want using a photocopier.

2 Cut out the shape. Put it on a piece of card and draw round it. Do this three times.

3 Cut out all three copies. Decorate the sides that will face out.

4 Fold them down the middle and stick or staple them together as shown in the diagrams.

❂ **Worksheets**

Worksheets ✪

Angel mobile

What you need

- white card
- scissors
- felt tips, paint, glitter, metallic paper, etc.
- glue
- thread

1   Cut out the angel. Put it on a piece of card, draw round it and cut out the copy.

2   Repeat with the wing, making two copies.

3   Decorate both sides of the wings and the front of the angel.

4   Fold the wings along the dotted line. Glue the striped tabs and fix them to the angel's back as shown in the diagram.

5   Thread cotton through the head to hang up your angel.

diagram

3-D star

What you need

- card
- scissors
- metallic paper
- glue
- thread
- glitter (optional)

1   Cut out the star. Put it on a piece of card, draw round it and cut out the copy.

2   Do this two more times, so you have three stars.

3   Cover the stars with metallic paper.

4   Fold two of the stars as shown in the diagram and stick the folded stars either side of the unfolded star.

5   Thread cotton through a point of the unfolded star to hang it up.

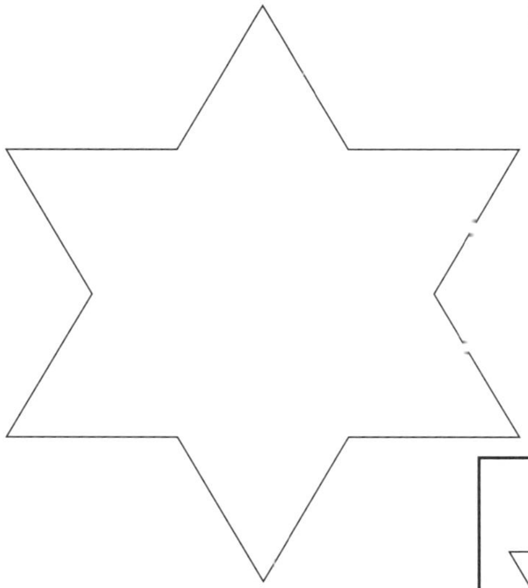

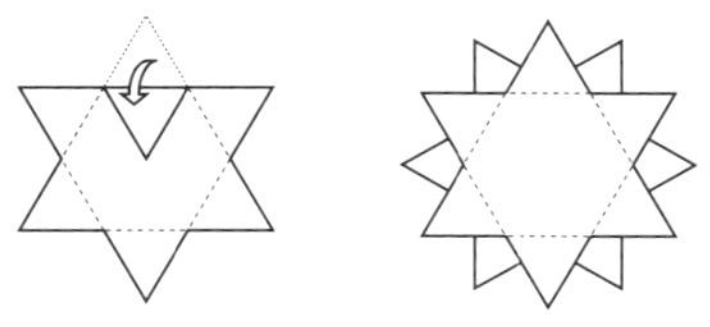

diagram

Pot pourri

What you need

- felt
- scissors
- needle and thread
- ribbon
- pot pourri mix

1 Choose a shape and cut it out. Put it on a piece of felt and cut around it.

2 Do this again so you have two copies.

3 Place the two copies back to back and sew them together. Leave the side marked 'x' open. Decorate if you want to.

4 Fill with pot pourri mix and sew up the top. Then sew on a loop of ribbon.

5 Put it in a plastic bag to keep fresh until you give it to someone as a present.

Leave this end open until filled

Leave this end open until filled

Leave this end open until filled

Finger puppets

What you need

- felt
- scissors
- needle and thread
- decoration materials
- felt tips

1 Cut out the puppet shape. Put it on a piece of felt and cut around it.

2 Do this again so you have two copies.

3 Place the two halves back to back and sew together, leaving the bottom open for your finger.

4 Sew on decorations and draw details to make the puppet into a Christmas character.

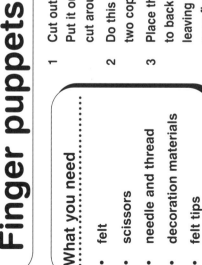

diagram

⭐ Worksheets

Spinning mobile

What you need

- coloured card
- scissors
- metallic paper and decorating materials
- glue
- needle and thread

1 Cut out one of the shapes. Put it on a piece of card, draw round it and cut out the copy.

2 Fold the card down the middle and cut round the shape of the inner line.

3 Decorate the inner and outer pieces then sew them together at the top.

4 Thread cotton through the top of the outer piece to hang up your mobile.

Jumpin' Santa

What you need

- card
- scissors
- small split pins
- thin string
- thread
- cotton wool, felt tips, etc. for decorating

1 Cut out the body shape. Put it on a piece of card, draw round it and cut out the copy.

2 Do this twice with the arms and legs.

3 Decorate Santa's face and costume.

4 Make holes carefully in the places shown and push the split pins through the body from the front.

5 Attach the arms and legs to the body as shown, then attach the string.

6 Hang up your Santa using the thread and pull the string to make him jump!

diagrams

Santa's sweet factory

What you need

- **cardboard tube**
- **scissors**
- **glue**
- **card**
- **felt tips, cotton wool, etc. for decorating**
- **red felt**
- **needle and thread**
- **sweets**

1. Cut the cardboard tube to the length you want your dispenser to be.

2. Draw round the base of the tube on card.

3. Draw a 1cm bigger circle around this and make cuts to inner circle. See diagram 1.

4. Fold up the tabs formed by the cuts and glue the outer edges. Insert into the base of the tube like a plug.

5. Measure, cut out and stick red felt around the tube. Decorate the tube to look like Santa.

6. Make a hat by sewing together two pieces of felt like the one shown. Measure half way round the tube and add $1\frac{1}{2}$ cm to find the right size for the opening. See diagram 2.

7. Fill the tube with sweets and put the hat on top.

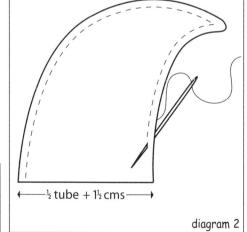

←— ½ tube + 1½ cms —→

diagram 2

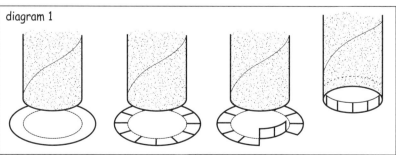

diagram 1

★ Worksheets

All you need for Christmas

Christmas cards

What you need

- **scissors**
- **A4 card**
- **paperclips**
- **tissue paper, felt tips, glitter, etc. to decorate**

Try these shaped cards this Christmas. They're easy to make but take care only to cut in the right places!

1 Choose a design and enlarge it on a photocopier. Then cut it out.

2 Fold a sheet of A4 card in half with the fold on the left and place the design on top.

3 Line up the bottom of design with the bottom of card. Then line up the left side of the design with the fold and fix it in place with paperclips.

4 Cut around the design. Decorate the card and write a message on the inside.

On the front of this card, cut out the window shapes and stick tissue paper on the inside for a stained glass effect

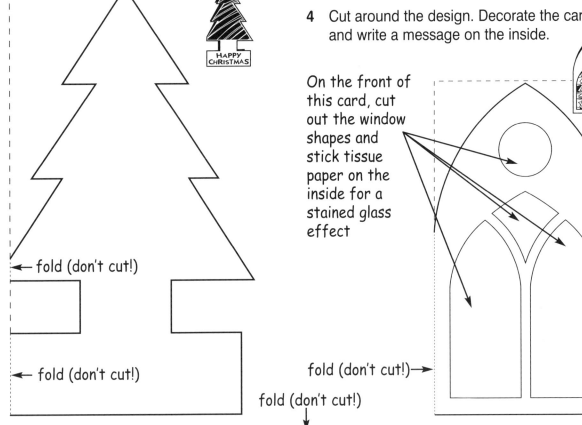

← fold (don't cut!)

← fold (don't cut!)

fold (don't cut!) →

fold (don't cut!)

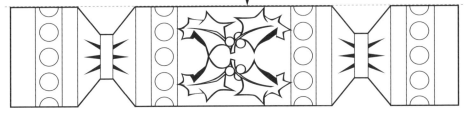

Use pinking shears for the ends of the cracker

Use pinking shears for the ends of the cracker

Worksheets ✪

Christmas card challenge

What you need

- A4 card
- pencil
- scissors
- decorating materials

These designs will create a 3-D stable scene or the inside of a church.

1 Select one of the designs shown.

2 Mark out the dimensions shown below on your card and then cut it out and fold along the broken lines.

3 Decorate the stable or church on the inside and the outside. Write your message on the back.

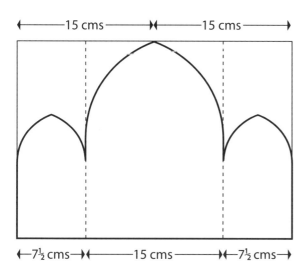

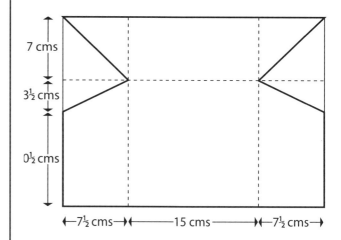

Design challenge

If you have selected the stable scene, make characters and animals which 'pop out' and move into a new position when the card is opened.

For the church scene, create a vicar and choir or congregation that do the same!

❖ **Worksheets**

ICT brainwaves

Write Christmas stories using at least eight sentences. Jumble the sentences up. See if others in the class can sort them out.

Draw a Christmas scene using Paint or a similar program.

Make Christmas cards for display before taking them home.

Produce a newspaper keeping the school up to date with the Christmas story. Use a range of multimedia resources – for example videos, OHTs, printed format – to give daily bulletins to the class or school.

Use Logo to generate a Christmas pattern – perhaps a star. Use the pattern to make a mobile.

Make cartoon picture series of Christmas tales.

Use a word processor to write wish lists to Father Christmas. Put festive borders around them.

Visit other school websites to see what they do for Christmas. Give an assembly on the findings. Keep the school website up to date with all your Christmas activities.

Scan photographs of the children and change the way they look. Colour hair festive green and send them home!

Set up a twinning arrangement with a school abroad. Find out how they celebrate Christmas, find pen pals, etc.

Make some Christmas acrostics using Word or Publisher. Change the colour of the key letters.

Using the Internet, investigate the origins of holly, ivy, mistletoe and fir as Christmas decorations. Report your findings using a multimedia presentation.

ICT ✪

Christmas party games 1

We all know many party games, but when it comes to brainstorming the Christmas party, somehow they disappear from our minds. Here are some ideas which you may like to try. They can be easily adapted.

One angry king

This is a variation of 'One fat hen'. One child starts by saying 'One angry king'. The next child repeats the first and then goes on to number two, eg. 'One angry king, Two tired donkeys,' and so on. Each line must concern some aspect of Christmas and each participant must repeat all the previous phrases before adding their own. There are no winners – the fun is in the confusion!

Miming can assist children with special needs.

You could make the game alliterative with, for example, 'One kind king, Two sad shepherds…'

Prancer

Children sit in a large circle and are each given the name of one of Santa's reindeer – Rudolph, Prancer, etc. The adult sits in the centre and calls out the name of one of the reindeer. All the children who have been given that name run or walk clockwise around the outside of the circle, trying to catch the person in front.

All 'caught' deer are out but should return to their sitting positions within the circle. They do not get up again in that game. The winners are the  children who are the only ones left in their groups at the end.

Christmas islands

Using the names of Christmas characters as group names, put each child into a group. Tape pieces of paper or card onto the floor as 'islands' with the name of a group on each piece of paper. Start with enough islands for everybody and gradually reduce the number. The children dance to music. When the music stops, the adult in charge calls out the name of a group, for example Kings. All the children in that group race for the islands labelled Kings. Only one child is allowed per island. Those not on an island are out, and so are any children who on wrong islands.

You could call out more than one group at a time, for example Kings and Shepherds.

Crazy Christmas

Starting with a few simple commands, this can develop into a frenetic game to suit all abilities. Children respond to agreed commands which are all related to Christmas (eg. 'Wait for Santa' means lie on the floor, 'Get the sacks' means go to the window, 'On the sledge' means sit on the floor, 'Icicle' means stand still and so on). After a few trial runs, the last one to respond is out, and so are any who make mistakes!

This is a rather noisy game, so have a quiet one ready as soon as it ends.

★ **Games and fun**

All you need for (**Christmas**)

Christmas party games 2

Christmas Kim's game

A good 'calming' game. Organise 12 or more Christmas-related objects on a tray. Equip all participants with pencil and paper. Give them one minute to observe the objects, then cover the tray and instruct the children to write down the names of as many objects as possible. Then stop them, swap papers and mark by going through the items. Do not penalise poor spelling as it is a game. Any object on a list that was not on the tray means minus a point. The winner is the child with the highest score. Develop the number or complexity of the objects in line with ability.

Christmas bells

One player leaves the room. Others stand in a circle, one with a small bell. The player returns to the middle of the circle, closes their eyes and is turned around twice by an adult. While the player is turning, the bell is tinkled. The player has to guess which child holds the bell behind their back. If the player guesses successfully, they change places for the next round. If not, the player has one more guess before they are replaced.

You could use two bells simultaneously for older children – and call it Stereo Bells.

Sleeping Santa

Story: The elves (children) want to escape the factory to play, but Santa has locked the door and gone to sleep with the keys beside him.

'Santa' is blindfolded and the rest of the children sit in a circle around him. The adult selects an 'elf' to creep up and take the keys without detection. Santa has one

chance to point in the direction where he thinks the elf is. The elf must then freeze while the adult decides if Santa is pointing at the elf. If Santa is correct, the keys are returned and another elf is selected. If the elf wins, then they become Santa.

Ensure Santa changes anyway after two or three tries.

Santa's sticky pans

Story: The elves have been fooling around again. While they were out playing, all the chocolate, toffee and sweets melted in the pans. The elves have run off and Santa has to catch them to sort out the mess.

Mark out 'pans' in paper 1m in diameter on the floor. The number will depend on the space available. A Santa is selected and identified out in some way. Santa must catch the elves and take them to the pans. Once in the pans, the elves can reach out and stick to other elves, so trapping them, too. Their feet must stay inside the pan and no elf may become unstuck and run off. Have rules where the children can only run, skip or walk. The last elf uncaught becomes the next Santa.

Games and fun ✪

Christmas quizzes

1 In which town was Jesus born?

2 Who was the mother of Jesus?

3 What building was Jesus born in?

4 What did his mother lay him in?

5 Who came to visit Jesus first?

6 Who came next?

7 Who followed a star?

8 Who saw an angel in the hills?

---

1 What were the names of the Three Wise Men?

2 What other title are they sometimes given?

3 Who advised them and why?

4 What does 'Messiah' mean?

5 Why did the Wise Men visit Herod?

6 What was their reaction to Herod's plan?

7 What is a census?

8 Why did the Roman emperor call a census?

9 Why were the Romans involved?

10 Why did the crowds in Bethlehem go after a few days?

11 Mary and Joseph took Jesus to which country?

12 Is Christmas celebrated on the same date each year?

13 Is this the exact date of Christmas?

14 Have you been good enough to have a visit from Father Christmas this year?

---

1 What sort of tree is associated with Christmas?

2 What plant has a romantic use at Christmas time?

3 Name the plant that has prickly leaves and red berries.

4 What special songs are sung at this time of year?

5 Name two things you might have with turkey.

6 Name two things you will find in a cracker.

7 Name the gifts brought by the Three Wise Men.

8 Why do families and friends give each other presents?

9 What two plants are named in a well-known carol?

10 Which is better and why – a stocking or a pillow case?

---

1 Name Mary's husband.

2 Where did Mary and Joseph live?

3 Name the angel.

4 Name the Three Wise Men.

5 What did the angel tell Mary?

6 Who was Herod?

7 Where did Herod live?

8 What did he tell the Wise Men to do?

9 What did the Wise Men do?

10 What is the date of Christmas Day?

★ **Games and fun**

Christmas riddles

What am I?

Wrap me up, just for show
To open me you'll not be slow!

I come in the night
But I cause no fright.

Under me you can steal a kiss
It's an opportunity you must not miss.

I'm filled with all sorts of things
Who knows what Santa will bring?

I go on display
And am then thrown away.

I've got a nose that's red
And I pull a sled.

You pull me apart
And your meal you start!

Birds feed on me
After your festivities.

You hang me here you hang me there
At Christmas hang me any-old-where!

Who am I?

His birth made me cross
If I win, it's your loss!

He was born for you and born for me
And born to set his people free.

The town was full – a B&B boom –
But in the end I found them room.

I went to the shepherds after seeing Mary
And, boy, they found me really scary.

I was the guy who could read the signs
Who read the books and made the finds.

Few people knew but I carried the mother
Over one hill and then another!

I was the man chosen to wed
The Lady of God, just like the man said!

I don't know why but He's chosen me
To be the mother, and do I agree?

Sitting on the ground we saw a bright light
And raced down the hill for a wonderful sight.

Games and fun ✪

Christmas wordsearch 1

Find the words from the list in the grid. Some words go across and some go down.

P	A	R	T	I	E	S	T	U	F	U	N
R	U	C	A	R	D	S	M	I	L	N	G
E	N	M	S	T	O	C	K	I	N	G	S
S	W	N	A	E	S	M	I	E	G	S	C
E	R	E	N	T	R	E	F	O	O	D	R
N	A	O	T	R	E	E	F	O	T	E	A
T	P	D	A	E	C	O	R	A	U	O	C
S	M	T	I	N	S	E	L	H	R	A	K
S	T	H	A	N	K	S	O	U	K	L	E
S	M	I	L	E	S	M	N	R	E	T	R
S	I	N	B	D	H	A	P	P	Y	E	S
D	E	C	O	R	A	T	I	O	N	S	C

PARTIES	**CRACKERS**	**TINSEL**
PRESENTS	**STOCKINGS**	**HAPPY**
FUN	**CARDS**	**UNWRAP**
FOOD	**TURKEY**	**THANKS**
SANTA	**DECORATIONS**	**SMILES**
	TREE	

★ **Games and fun**

Christmas wordsearch 2

Find the words from the list in the grid. They go in all directions – up, down, forwards, backwards and diagonally.

B	S	H	P	E	S	O	J	E	S	U	S	E	H
L	E	G	N	A	G	O	H	R	R	Y	M	S	O
J	J	T	W	A	R	T	S	A	T	O	E	N	L
E	A	S	H	P	R	C	T	O	M	J	L	E	Y
R	N	B	A	L	T	H	A	Z	A	R	C	C	I
U	I	D	U	L	E	D	B	S	D	S	H	N	S
S	S	T	O	C	B	H	L	E	P	C	I	I	D
A	M	T	A	N	G	N	E	H	L	A	O	K	R
L	F	E	E	R	K	A	U	M	V	B	R	N	E
E	P	R	A	H	R	E	B	A	S	M	I	A	H
M	A	T	E	P	P	H	Y	R	D	A	K	R	P
E	S	R	J	D	L	O	G	Y	I	L	R	F	E
A	O	G	I	F	T	S	R	H	A	E	N	M	H
D	H	A	I	S	S	E	M	P	O	L	L	T	S

BETHLEHEM	**CASPAR**	**MESSIAH**	**HEROD**
JOSEPH	**JOY**	**STABLE**	**PEACE**
JESUS	**BALTHAZAR**	**SHEPHERDS**	**MARY**
MELCHIOR	**PROPHETS**	**GIFTS**	**GABRIEL**
ANGEL	**JERUSALEM**	**FRANKINCENSE**	**LAMB**
MYRRH	**STRAW**	**GOLD**	**HOLY**
	DONKEY	**STAR**	

Games and fun ✪

Christmas crossword 1

Across

1 One of the kings [6]

3 A Christmas hymn [5]

5 Advisor to the Wise Men [10]

9 Jesus is the Son of ___ [3]

10 A king who feared any rivals [5]

13 A gift from the shepherds [4]

14 ___ Lord, Jesus Christ [3]

15 He provided shelter [9]

Down

1 Baby Jesus [6,5]

2 The Wise Men followed one [4]

4 Be near me ___ Jesus [4]

6 Mary and Joseph lived there [8]

7 One of the gifts [4]

8 Another of the kings [8]

11 Jesus gives his ___ [4]

12 Mother of Jesus [4]

☆ Games and fun

Christmas crossword 2

Across

1 A good feeling [5]

4 The Christmas angels brought great ___ [3]

5 Do this properly when eating your Christmas dinner! [4]

7 When to look at your stocking on Christmas morning [5]

8 The donkey stood while ___ burden alighted [3]

9 Jesus lay in a sort of ___ [4]

12 A kind of donkey [3]

13 When the angel came to the shepherds [5]

15 Do we love Jesus? [3]

16 It helped the Wise Men [4]

19 The City of David [9]

20 The shepherds gazed in ___ [3]

21 When it's snowing, it certainly isn't ___ ! [3]

22 Dangerous, but giving a soft light [7]

24 And __, the angel appeared [2]

25 When Herod said what he was going to do it was a ___ [3]

26 A soft light was _____ in the stable [7]

Down

1 Time off from school [7]

2 What we hope to have if we've been good! [8]

3 We often think the weather will be ___ at Christmas [3]

6 People in church [11]

10 Jesus came to us as a ____ [4]

11 Christians go to this, especially at Christmas time [6]

14 The shepherds were glad of it [4]

17 Funny place to be born! [6]

18 Mary was the _____ of God [6]

19 '__ not afraid,' said the angel [2]

21 Joseph, Mary and Jesus are the ____ family [4]

23 When is the time to love Jesus? [3]

Curriculum activities planner

Geography/History

ICT

Maths

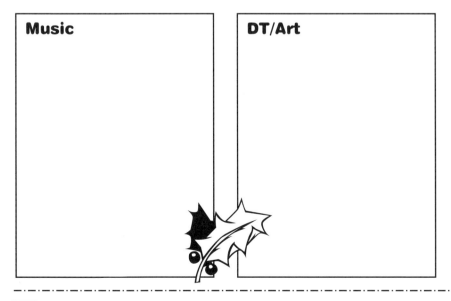

RE

PE

Dance

English

Drama

Music

DT/Art

Science

★ **Planning templates**

All you need for Christmas

School events weekly planner

For week commencing

	Morning activities	Time	Staff in charge	Afternoon activities	Time	Staff in charge	Evening activities	Time	Staff in charge
MON									
TUE									
WED									
THU									
FRI									

Christmas party planner

Class .... **Date** .... **Time** ....

Timings	Activities and location	Resources (inc. adults)	To do	✔
Health and Safety plus Special Needs considerations				

⭐ **Planning templates**

Party letter for parents

CHRISTMAS PARTY

Dear Parents,

The Christmas Party/ies will be held on .... December at ....pm.

We always appreciate the contributions you make towards the success of these occasions and would be grateful if you could indicate below the type(s) of food you are able to provide.

Your child should bring the items to school on the morning of the party and deliver them to the class teacher.

If you are able to assist staff in running the party please complete the line below and return the form to school as soon as possible.

Thank you in anticipation for helping to make this year's party a great success!

Yours sincerely,

✂ --

Name of child..

I will be able to provide

Savoury items	Sweet items	Drink

I will be able to help run the Christmas Party this term. YES/NO

I would particularly like to help with: ....

Name (please print) ....

Special events planner

Event _____

Date _____ Time _____ Year groups involved _____

Activities and organisation	Staff in charge	Resources	Action required	✔

Health and Safety plus Special Needs considerations

⭐ **Planning templates**

Did you know...?

Christmas

The word is short for Christ's Mass – or birthday. We celebrate it on 25 December but that's not the true date. He was actually born in March, as far as we can tell. The date of 25 December was chosen around the middle of the fourth century, possibly to replace the pagan festival of Yule at the winter solstice (which celebrated the lengthening of days) and the Roman Saturnalia (which celebrated the returning power of the sun). It's thought that early Christians may have persuaded others that the light of Christ was more powerful than anything else, so they gradually converted to Christianity.

Christmas crackers

A British invention! Tom Smith from Clerkenwell, London is the man to thank for these! He brought back the idea of bon-bons from Paris in 1840. He had the idea of adding two strips of card joined by saltpetre so that there would be a little 'cracking' explosion when the wrappers were opened. He called them Cosaques after the crack of the whips used by Cossack horsemen.

They eventually had larger wrappings and contained other things than a bon-bon. The cracker was born!

Mistletoe

Kiss, kiss! Actually, in pagan times, enemies who met under mistletoe had to declare a truce until the next day, such were its supposed magical powers. In a sense, kissing under mistletoe is a continuation of this peaceful theme.

In Portugal...

People often use shoes instead of stockings. Not very fair if you only have little feet!

The Portuguese have a feast called 'consoada' on Christmas Day at which they set extra places at the table for 'alminhas a penar' (the souls of the dead). Sounds fun.

Reindeer

We all know that Father Christmas's reindeer are magic reindeer because they can fly, but we don't always remember their names which are Rudolph, Blitzen, Comet, Cupid, Dancer, Dasher, Donner, Prancer and Vixen. The names were first published in 1822 by Clement Clark Moore, an American poet.

In some countries, reindeer don't get a look in. There, Santa is assisted by a white horse, a mule, or even a goat!

Christmas cards

The first card was designed in London in 1840 by John Calcott Horsley. It went on sale in 1843. A thousand were produced at one shilling each – that was quite a lot of money!

Father Christmas first appeared on a card in America. Abraham Lincoln asked Thomas Nast to illustrate Santa Claus with the Union troops to cheer them up during the Civil War. He was dressed in blue.